# HOW TO WRITE A TERM PAPER

# HOW TO WRITE A TERM PAPER

## CYNTHIA KEYWORTH

**Arco Publishing, Inc.**
**New York**

Published by Arco Publishing, Inc.
219 Park Avenue South, New York, N.Y. 10003

Copyright © 1982 by Cal Industries, Inc.

**Library of Congress Cataloging in Publication Data**

Keyworth, Cynthia.
     How to write a term paper.

     1. Dissertations, Academic.     I. Title.
LB2369.K46      808′.02      81-22761
ISBN 0-668-05321-6 (pbk.)      AACR2

Printed in the United States of America

# Contents

# HOW TO WRITE A TERM PAPER

# Introduction

A term paper is a composition based on research done in a library. Writing a term paper teaches you how to research a subject, organize reference material, and use footnotes and a bibliography. This book will take you through the process of writing a term paper by giving you step-by-step explanations, examples, and useful teach-yourself tests.

Writing a term paper will help you develop the writing skills you'll need in school and for the rest of your life. In school for example, you may need to check a date for a history class, read a book review for English, organize material for an essay exam, and write compositions for your classes. In your personal and work life, research and writing skills are also very important. Some day you may need to get facts for a report you are giving to the P.T.A. or your tenants' association. You may need to write a memo to your boss on working conditions in your office. You may need background information on makes of cars, household appliances, and furniture before buying them. Writing a term paper teaches you the basic skills to perform these tasks. It is, therefore, as much a learning experience as a writing one.

One of the advantages of writing a term paper is that it is done in steps. Each step along the way provides a chance to improve your skills in research, organization and writing.

**Research.** You'll learn that the library is a resource for many kinds of information. You'll learn how to get that information easily. You'll also learn how to use a card catalogue and reference books, and how to find articles in magazines.

**Organization.** You'll learn that the outline is a powerful tool. The outline organizes your paper according to major ideas. It puts those ideas in the correct order. It lets you write your paper without panic *because it shows you where you are going*.

**Writing.** Because the actual writing experience builds on what you've already done, you needn't dread this final task. You'll know that you've thoroughly researched your subject and have a strong outline to guide you.

All research and writing begin by asking questions. Knowing the right questions, therefore, is as important as knowing the right answers. Writing a term paper will teach you how to ask the right questions. When you've neared the end of your research, you will be able to answer the questions to your satisfaction and formulate a thesis statement, or central idea. A term paper, then, is the writer's answer to a question, supported by evidence.

# Planning Your Term Paper

## *Choosing A Subject*

There are two general rules for choosing a subject. First, a subject must have been the subject of serious research. If your subject can only be found in news magazines, for example, and not in books or serious articles, it isn't suitable. Second, be sure you have enough sources to work with. A minimum of 8 or 10 books and articles is acceptable.

Certain subjects are not suitable for a term paper. You should *avoid* subjects which are:

- *Too recent to have much information.* Certain current events are too recent to provide you with sources other than newspaper articles. You won't be able to use reference books and research articles.

- *Too regional or specialized to have much information.* For example, you may be interested in your city's method of purifying water, or its early history. But unless there is enough reference material available, these topics won't be suitable.

- *Too emotional to be treated objectivly.* Some subjects, like gun control, are simply too hot to handle in a term paper. Perhaps rightly, since they bring forth very emotional reactions. You may be faced with balancing conflicting opinions, even conflicting facts.

- *Too complex to judge accurately.* Some subjects require special knowledge. For example, you probably aren't equipped to judge current theories about nuclear fusion.

If you are writing a term paper for an English or composition course, you may be free to decide your own subject. The following four methods will help you come up with a worthwhile and interesting one.

1. **Begin with your favorite school subject.** Let's say you've taken an American history course which you enjoyed. You remember reading something about Theodore Roosevelt, who had a career as a statesman, naturalist, conservationist, soldier, writer, and President. Following are some notes and questions you might jot down which would lead you to an appropriate subject.

> Theodore Roosevelt
>    His life.
>    Too broad to be the basis of a term paper.
>
>    What was T.R.'s effect on big business?
>    What was his role in the Spanish-American War?
>    Didn't he leave a Cabinet position to become a soldier? How important were the Rough Riders, the group Roosevelt led into battle?

2. **Write about your hobbies or special interests.** What do you like to do best? What do you like to read about? What documentary subjects interested you on television? The following is a list one student made.

> Sports
>    Role in universities? Politics of the Olympics?
>
> Playing the guitar
>    History of blues music? Origin of jazz?
>
> Cooking
>    Too informal. Something about nutrition?
>
> Science fiction
>    My English teacher mentioned last week that science fiction is taught in some schools—so there might be enough sources. Would be interesting to compare early science fiction with today's work. (Check with teacher and/or library.)

3. **Choose a subject based on a group to which you belong.** Your race, ethnic origin, economic class, place of residence, religious affiliation, or membership in an organization may provide special interests which you could write about in a term paper. The following is one student's list, accompanied by questions which could become term paper subjects.

> Catholic Church
>    Should federal aid to church schools be abolished? Should churches retain their tax exempt status?
>
> Chicano
>    Should public school courses be taught in Spanish? Are minority quotas fair?

State of Arizona

How will Arizona solve its water supply problem? Who should have water rights to the Colorado River? What are the obstacles to cleaning up air pollution caused by copper smelting? How much land should be reserved for national parks?

WARNING: Don't let your prejudices come between you and a good paper. If you're already committed to one side of an issue, or think you've got all the answers, you may end up with a lopsided, badly reasoned paper. *Don't write about something unless you can honestly set aside your biases. Examine the facts until you reach logical conclusions.*

4. **Make other people's ideas work for you.** Pay attention to special documentaries on television. Leaf through new books. Read the editorial page of a major newspaper like *The New York Times*. Scan the table of contents in magazines, reading the titles and one-line descriptions. Magazine articles are usually limited in scope and will help you both choose and limit a subject.

If you are in a class in which you are asked to develop a term paper in that field, your range of choices has already been narrowed for you. The following three hints will help you find a subject under those circumstances.

1. Review your semester's notes. Are there some questions for which you never found the answers? Was some person or event or idea particularly interesting?

2. If your teacher provided the class with a list of required or supplemental readings, re-read it. Are there some titles of books or articles which give you an idea for a subject?

3. If you can, connect what interests you with the term-paper course. If you like math and you're taking a social science course, you might look at the impact of computers on some aspect of society. If you're interested in art and are taking a home economics course, you might study modern domestic architecture. If you like English and you're taking a psychology course, you might want to examine theories about the creative process.

## Limiting Your Subject

You cannot do justice to a subject that is too broad. A term paper must be focused and limited enough so that you can do a good job in 10 to 20 pages, within a reasonable amount of time, and with the research materials at your disposal.

Limiting your subject makes you more productive and improves your final paper. It is better to say a lot about a little than a little about a lot. As a matter of fact, choosing a subject and limiting it are really part of the same process. Right from the start, as you're hunting around for a good subject, you should be looking for ways to limit it.

The first step in limiting your subject is to *ask questions*. Write down a possible subject area. Then write down all the questions you can think of about that subject. Write down every question, from the most obvious to the most far-flung. Each question will focus on a limited aspect of the subject. Here are two examples:

United Nations
    How was it begun?
    For what purpose? Does it achieve its purpose?
    What are its functions?
    Who belongs to it?
    Do small countries have the same vote as big countries?
    What is UNICEF?
    How do we choose ambassadors to the U.N.?
    Possible subject: The peace-keeping functions of the U.N.

Dreams
    Why do we dream?
    Do blind persons dream?
    What happens to a person when he can't dream?
    Why do we dream *what* we dream?
    Do dreams tell us something about ourselves?
    How do the mentally ill dream?
    Are children's dreams special in any way?
    What are nightmares? Are they necessary?
    Does stress or crisis affect dreaming?
    Why is it so difficult to remember our dreams?
    Possible subject: Comparison of special dreams: the dreams of
    the mentally ill, the blind, and of persons in crisis.

Another method of limiting your subject is to make it more specific. In the following examples, a general subject is made more specific—step-by-step.

Psychology
    Animal behavior
        Chimpanzee behavior
            Chimpanzee learning ability
                Chimpanzee ability to learn sign language

Religion
    Christianity
        Christian texts
            Non-Biblical texts
                Dead Sea Scrolls

1. Limit the following broad subjects by asking yourself a series of questions.

   Secondary education
   U.S. Theatre
   Immigration
   The Antarctic
   Cancer research

2. Using four or five steps, make each subject listed above more specific.

Not only must you limit the scope of your subject, you must give it *time limits*. Knowing the time limits of something is an important way of defining and understanding it. You must know when things began—school integration, Ford's presidency, television, jazz, strip mining. And you must know when things ended—the Vietnam War, Prohibition, Shakespeare's last play.

Set limits on the history you will examine. If you're researching safety improvements on automobiles, decide what your time limits are; for example, 1950 to the present. Setting time limits naturally limits your subject and limits the research you will do.

Know exactly what you mean when you use words and phrases like *contemporary, modern, recent, long ago*. When appropriate, share your meaning with your readers by providing dates.

**EXAMPLES.** Sometimes time spans are not exact, for example, the civil rights movement. Sometimes they are very precise, for example, the reign of Queen Victoria. In either case, they are important. The writer of the following phrases must understand clearly the time spans they suggest:

The rise of the automobile        Modern art
Rock and roll music               Recent Supreme Court decisions
The Depression                    Ancient superstitions

# Research And Note Taking

## General Reference Works

You will probably begin your research by doing some preliminary reading in *general reference books*. These books are found in the reference section of your library. As a rule, they cannot be checked out. They include encyclopedias, dictionaries, atlases, yearbooks on current events, guides to literature, and so forth. You should familiarize yourself with the reference books in your area of study and learn where they are in the library.

Constance Winchell's *Guide to Reference Books,* 8th edition, can direct you to helpful sources. It provides a brief description of reference books in the following areas: General Reference Works, The Humanities, Social Sciences, History and Area Studies, Pure and Applied Science. If, for example, the subject of your term paper is opera, you would look in the Humanities section under music. There, you will find nine reference works under Opera, including an encyclopedia of opera, a dictionary of opera terms, and a catalog of operas on American subjects. The description of each work will let you see at a glance whether the work will be useful.

General reference works can be excellent sources, particularly for background information. But their articles are often too brief and not analytical enough to form the bulk of your final paper. Only a small percentage of your cited material should come from general references.

## The Card Catalog

The next research step is to use the library's card catalog. It contains an alphabetical listing of all library holdings by *author's name* and *title of publication*. Non-fiction books are also listed under *subject* headings. Review the following samples of author, title and subject cards found in the card catalog.

## AUTHOR CARD

Call numbers
tell you where
to find the book

Author

Title

Publication
information

Subject head-
ings under
which you can
find this book
listed by
subject
Check here for
related books

Library
classifications

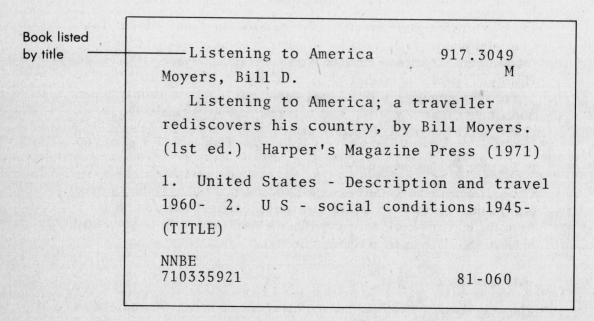

917.3049

Moyers, Bill D.
   Listening to America; a traveller
rediscovers his country, by Bill Moyers.
(1st ed.)  Harper's Magazine Press (1971)

1.  United States - Description and travel
1960-  2.  U S - social conditions 1945-
(TITLE)

NNBE
710335921
                     81-060

## TITLE CARD

Book listed
by title

   Listening to America   917.3049
Moyers, Bill D.             M
   Listening to America; a traveller
rediscovers his country, by Bill Moyers.
(1st ed.)  Harper's Magazine Press (1971)

1.  United States - Description and travel
1960-  2.  U S - social conditions 1945-
(TITLE)

NNBE
710335921
                     81-060

Book listed
by subject

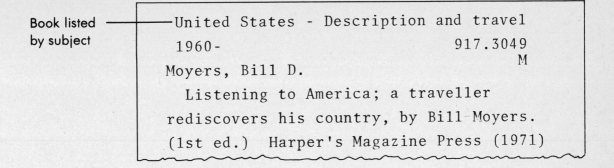

```
United States - Description and travel
1960-                              917.3049
                                          M
Moyers, Bill D.
   Listening to America; a traveller
rediscovers his country, by Bill Moyers.
(1st ed.)  Harper's Magazine Press (1971)
```

Subject cards are probably the first place you'll look during the early stages of your research. Therefore, begin by making a list of the possible subject areas for your paper, and pay close attention to the cross-references in the card catalog.

**Note:** Some librarians now use computer printout catalog instead of cards. The information and format of the entry is the same; however, the material is set on pages and bound like a book. Usually, there are three book catalogs: for author, title, and subject.

## Indexes to Periodicals and Newspapers

Periodical indexes are your guides to magazines and newspapers. The following four indexes will be useful.

1. *Reader's Guide to Periodical Literature.* 1900—

This is an index to over 300 general American periodicals, such as *Vital Speeches, Congressional Digest, American Heritage, Scientific American, The New Yorker, Parents,* and *Natural History.* It lists published articles by author and subject; reviews of ballets, books, drama, movies, theatre, opera, records, and television programs are also indexed.

SAMPLE ENTRY

HALL, Donald
   On the third hand.    N Y Times Bk R
   84:25+    Ap 29 '79

**Explanation:** Donald Hall's article "On the Third Hand," appeared in *The New York Times Book Review* on April 29, 1979. It will be found in volume number 84 on page 25 and succeeding pages.

DREAMS

Dreams.   J. Ogle.   il Vogue 169:491 S '79

**Explanation:** One of the articles listed under the subject heading Dreams is J. Ogle's article, called "Dreams." It is illustrated and appeared in *Vogue* magazine in September 1979, and will be found in volume 169 on page 491.

2.  *Social Science Index* and *Humanities Index*. 1965—
    Formerly *Social Science and Humanities Index*. 1958.65.
    Formerly *International Index*. 1907.1958.

These are indexes to scholarly and technical journals. Consult the *Humanities Index* for articles on art, literature, philosophy, and religion. Consult the *Social Science Index* for articles on anthropology, archaeology, economics, geography, history, political science, and sociology.

SAMPLE ENTRY

THERMOPYLAE, Battle of, 480 B.C.
    Anopaia path at Thermopylia. P.W.
    Wallace.
        il map Am J Archaeol 84:15-23 Ja '80

An illustrated article with map on the subject of the battle of Thermopylai entitled
"Anopaia path at Thermopylai," by
P.W. Wallace, will be found in volume
84 of American Journal of Archaeology,
pages 15-23, the January 1980 number

3.  *The New York Times Index*. 1851—

By its own classification, this index "...presents a condensed, classified history of the world as it is recorded day-by-day in *The New York Times*." Entries are made under subject headings and consist of summaries of news and editorials. The Index gives precise information—by date, page and column—to the item it summarizes. You may use the summaries themselves, or you may use the index to locate the original article. All but the most recent issues of *The New York Times* are stored on microfilm and will be found in the microfilm room of a library. Microfilm is easy to use. The librarian will be glad to instruct you.

In this index, headings and subheadings are arranged alphabetically, but arrangement *within* entries is chronological. So, if you look up "Iran" in the 1979 volume of the Index, you will find twenty-one pages of the *Times*'s day-to-day coverage of Iran, a useful mini-history.

If you look at "Education and Schools—U.S." under the subheading "Drop-outs," you will find the entry listed below.

## SAMPLE ENTRY

Labor Dept begins experimental program to encourage poor youths to finish h s by guaranteeing them jobs part-time during school yr and full-time during summer (S), S 18, 47:1

**Explanation:** A short (S) article on discouraging youths from dropping out of high school appeared in the *Times* on September 18, on page 47, column 1. (The six columns are numbered right to left.)

4. *Biography Index.* 1946—

This index lists full-length biographies, as well as biographical material appearing in books, magazines, obituaries, diaries, memoirs, collections of letters, and bibliographies. Entries are listed by subject (that is, by person). If you look under Shakespeare in Volume 11, you will find twenty-six books and articles listed. One of them is shown below.

## SAMPLE ENTRY

Schoenbaum, Samuel. William Shakespeare: a compact documentary life. abr ed Oxford '77 376 pp bibl il pors facsims autog

**Explanation:** Samuel Schoenbaum is the author of *William Shakespeare: A Compact Documentary Life,* an abbreviated edition published by Oxford University Press in 1977. The book, which has 376 pages, is illustrated and contains a bibliography, portraits, facsimiles reproductions of documents and the playwright's autograph.

The four preceding indexes are the most widely used. However, the following additional indexes may also be useful. The words in parentheses tell how the information is listed.

*Agricultural Index.* 1919. 1964
  *Biological and Agricultural Index.* 1964—
    (Subject)

*Applied Science and Technology Index.* 1958—
  (Subject)

*The Art Index.* 1929—
  (Author, Subject)

*Book Review Digest.* 1905—
  (Author, Title, Subject)

*Business Periodicals Index.* 1958—

*Education Index.* 1929—
  (Author, Subject)

*Engineering Index.* 1884—
  (Subject)

*Music Index.* 1949—
  (Subject)

*Nineteenth Century Readers' Guide.* 1890.99.
  (Author, Subject)

*Poole's Index to Periodical Literature.* 1802.1906.
  (Subject)

*Public Affairs Information Service.* 1915—
  (Subject)

---

**QUICK TEST**

In which indexes would you find entries for the following:

1. articles in *Newsweek*

2. obituary of Harry S. Truman

3. articles on anthropology before 1958

4. articles on Shakespeare's *Taming of the Shrew*

5. review of a book on the life of Walt Whitman

6. editorial reactions to Nixon's resignation

7. reviews of "All in the Family" TV series

---

## Compiling a Bibliography

For each publication you read and take notes from, you will make out a bibliography card. A bibliography is a list of publications used in researching and writing a term paper. It is an alphabetical listing by author, including publication data. In the note-taking stage, your bibliography begins with your collection of bibliography cards.

Bibliography cards and note cards should be made out on 3x5 or 4x6 index cards. Students sometimes find the large size more convenient because it can hold more information. The information on the card should appear exactly as it will in your final version. This is done for two reasons: (1) It helps you keep track of all pertinent information, editions, date of publication, etc.; and (2) It allows you to put the cards in alphabetical order and easily refer to them when you type up your final draft. If you have hastily or carelessly left off vital information, you'll have to go back to the library and hunt down the publication again.

Keep your bibliography cards separate from your note cards. The entries on a bibliography card are: (1) author's full name, last name first, (2) title in full, (3) place of publication, (4) publishing agent, (5) date of publication. Additional information, such as volume number, edition, etc., is often needed. For the correct bibliography form for different kinds of publications, see the examples in the chapter entitled "The Completed Paper." In addition, write down information which will be helpful to you. For example, record the call number for later reference, and note any comments about the book you've gained from the library card. These facts will be useful if you want to find and use the book again.

SAMPLE BIBLIOGRAPHY CARD

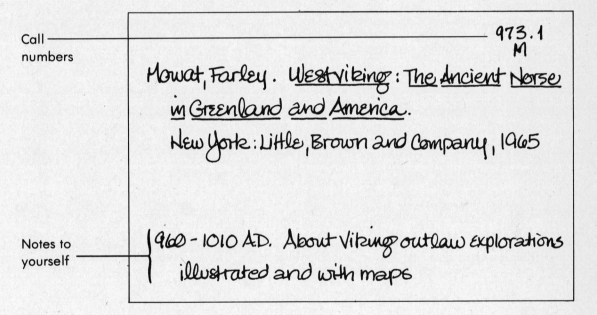

Call numbers

973.1
M

Mowat, Farley. West Viking: The Ancient Norse in Greenland and America.
New York: Little, Brown and Company, 1965

Notes to yourself

960 – 1010 A.D. About Viking outlaw explorations illustrated and with maps

## Evaluating Your Sources

One of your research jobs will be to choose sources which are best for your subject. The following questions will help you evaluate your sources:

- *Are they appropriate?* If you are studying some aspect of American foreign policy, *Time* or *Newsweek* may not provide articles with enough depth. However, if you're studying attitudes toward foreign policy, you might check news magazines for recent polls. Always look for serious, in-depth articles.

- *Are they biased, or prejudiced?* Look for biases in your sources. You will find biases in almost everything you read. They will range from strong prejudices which distort the facts to more gentlé leanings which favor one viewpoint over another. You must learn to judge whether the bias of an author makes his or her work unacceptable or unsound. You can make biases work for you by clearly identifying the source when you present the material and by presenting the opposing view.

- *Are they authoritative?* Check the author's credentials and education; read the preface or introduction to learn something of his or her methods, biases, and background. Try to determine the author's qualifications for writing the book or article. Find out what he or she has previously written. Find out what other people have thought of the author's book by consulting *Book Review Digest*. Book reviews are an excellent source, by the way, since the reviewer often discusses the content of the book.

- *Are they current?* For many studies, up-to-the-minute sources aren't necessary. For a literary term paper on Shakespeare's comedies, for example, you might use critical sources spanning nearly four hundred years. However, if you're dealing with a contemporary issue, you should read the latest published information and opinions. Even in dealing with historical matters, you'll want to see what is currently being written. Later scholars may have access to papers, data, or research that earlier ones did not.

## Reading Your Research Sources

Reading for a term paper differs from reading for entertainment and even from reading a textbook. It requires you to be active rather than passive, to make judgments and decisions.

Many students begin reading "cold." They plunge into reading and note-taking knowing little about its appropriateness, length, and scope. It's much better to scan an article or book before settling down to read it. Scanning a piece lets you know if it's suitable for your research. It makes the actual reading easier.

*Scanning gives you the "feel" of the work.* If you're reading a book, begin by looking at the Table of Contents. There you can quickly see how the book is organized and identify its major topics. Next, flip to the index and look up your subject and related subject areas. Read the preface or introduction and first paragraph to get an idea of the author's purpose, and possibly his thesis statement. Check for helpful aids like bibliographies, suggested reading lists, and tables and graphs. Look at the end of a chapter or the book for summaries. If you are reading an article, scan the section headings and read both the opening and closing paragraphs. Now you're more familiar with the work at hand, and will be better able to judge and read it.

## Producing Note Cards

Note taking is not merely a process of copying down someone else's words in your own handwriting. A researcher is not a stenographer. When you take notes, you do three important jobs:

1. **Select what is important and significant.** In everything you read, there will be much that is not useful to you. Ask yourself, "Will this piece of information help me answer my basic question?" There cannot always be a clear-cut answer, especially in the early stages of research. Remember that learning what to leave out as well as what to put in is a necessary skill.

2. **Summarize your material through paraphrasing.** To paraphrase is to say again in your own words. Just "saying again" isn't enough, however, you must also condense the material. When you condense you say again in fewer words. This is important because you can't put entire books and articles on note cards. Also, it helps you focus on what you really need.

   There are times when you'll want to use *direct quotations* instead of a summary. For example, when an author gives an apt definition or insight, or says something in an interesting way. If you are tempted to rely heavily on direct quotations, remember that your job is to analyze information, not to serve it up like a slice of pie. For that reason, many teachers don't like to see large chunks of quotations appearing frequently in a paper. Some will even ask that only ten per cent of the completed paper be in the form of direct quotations.

3. **Categorize your material under subject headings.** Each note card is identified by its subject. As you begin to sort out the major subject areas for your paper, you will soon have piles of note cards for each subject heading. Eventually these subject headings may become the major entries in your outline.

   The following are the characteristics of a well-done note card:

- It contains only one idea.

- It has a subject heading to identify the idea.

- It uses direct quotation only when necessary.

- It identifies the author and page number of the work from which the material was taken.

## SAMPLE NOTE CARDS

### DIRECT QUOTE

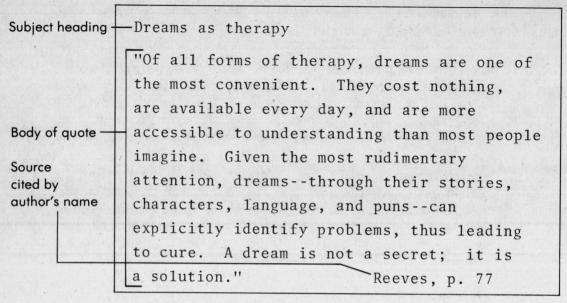

Subject heading — Dreams as therapy

Body of quote —

Source cited by author's name

"Of all forms of therapy, dreams are one of the most convenient.  They cost nothing, are available every day, and are more accessible to understanding than most people imagine.  Given the most rudimentary attention, dreams--through their stories, characters, language, and puns--can explicitly identify problems, thus leading to cure.  A dream is not a secret;  it is a solution."                    Reeves, p. 77

Later, to find the source, you need only go to your bibliography card for Reeve's book, filed alphabetically under "R".

### PARAPHRASE

Dreams as therapy

Dreams are a handy form of therapy--free available, and easily understood.  A dream can pinpoint problems and offer solutions.

Reeves, p. 77

```
Dreams as therapy

Dreams are "one of the most convenient"
kinds of therapy: free, available, and
easily understood.  A dream can pinpoint
problems--it "is not a secret; it is a
solution."


                              Reeves, p. 77
```

Not everything pertaining to your term paper will go on note cards. There may be occasions when you want to photocopy material—like tables, graphs, chronologies, or other listings. Remember that this material, if used, will have to be interpreted before it is included in your paper. As a general rule, it's better not to reproduce graphs or tables in a term paper. Present significant facts in the body of the paper, using your own words.

## TEACH YOURSELF
Paraphrase the main idea of the paragraph below.

A foolish consistency is the hobgoblin of little minds, adored by little statesmen and philosophers and divines. With consistency a great soul has simply nothing to do. He may as well concern himself with his shadow on the wall. Speak what you think now in hard words and tomorrow speak what tomorrow thinks in hard words again, though it contradict everything you said to-day.—'Ah, so you shall be sure to be misunderstood.'—Is it so bad then to be misunderstood? Pythagoras was misunderstood, and Socrates, and Jesus, and Luther, and Copernicus, and Galileo, and Newton, and every pure and wise spirit that ever took flesh. To be great is to be misunderstood.

—Ralph Waldo Emerson, "Self-Reliance"

# The Thesis Statement

*Thesis* comes from the Greek word meaning "proposition." You can think of the thesis statement as the idea you are proposing. It is the central idea of your paper, stated in a single, complete sentence. It defines the scope of your paper and determines the way you write your paper.

From the beginning of your research, you will be testing possible thesis statements. Midway through your research, you may formulate a tentative thesis statement which you will later use or discard. Or, you may wait until you've jotted down a rough outline before you produce an adequate thesis statement.

- *The thesis statement is just that — a statement.* It is *not* a question, and should not appear in question form.

  INCORRECT: Should commercial airline stewards receive stricter safety training?

  CORRECT: Commercial airline stewards should receive stricter safety training.

- *The thesis statement should be a complete sentence.* Don't confuse your title with your thesis. Your statement must have a subject and a verb to form a complete thought.

  INCORRECT: The role of Touchstone in Shakespeare's *As You Like it.*

  CORRECT: Touchstone plays the "wise fool" in *As You Like It.*

- *The thesis statement should contain only one idea.*

  INCORRECT: Early science fiction reflected an interest in great technological advances and portrayed women as one-dimensional and stereotyped.

  CORRECT: Early science fiction portrayed women as one-dimensional stereotypes.

- *The strongest thesis statements are specific, not vague and general.*

  ACCEPTABLE: Television advertising negatively affects children.

  BETTER: Television advertising for children gives them unrealistic desires by portraying a daily "Christmas morning" which appears to be easily obtainable.

- *A thesis statement should never be a simple personal response.*

WEAK: *Huckleberry Finn* is a fascinating account.

BETTER: The character of Huckleberry Finn has been seen as a symbol of the American spirit.

WEAK: There are many consequences of alchoholism.

BETTER: The social consequences of alchoholism are severe: it causes traffic deaths, medical deaths, loss of productivity, and raises insurance rates.

---

## QUICK TEST

What is the problem with each of the following thesis statements?

1. The theme of Walt Whitman's poetry is freedom of the individual; also his poetry influenced many other poets.

2. The meaning of the Declaration of Independence.

3. The themes in modern country music are interesting.

4. Social services in this country are being carefully examined.

5. In her novel *Cheri,* Colette presents a fascinating portrait.

6. What can we do about the fuel shortage?

---

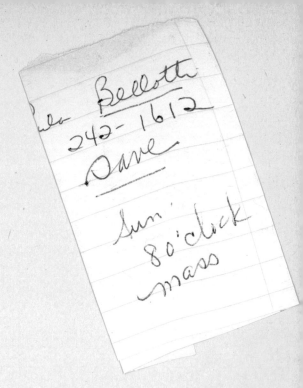

# The Outline

## *Introduction*

An outline shows the basic structure of your paper. It is like a skeleton which you will flesh out later. To prepare an outline, you must answer two questions: (1) What are the major ideas? (2) In what order do they belong?

Let's begin with an informal example of organizing ideas. The comments below were made by a man discussing a baseball game.

Bleacher seats are only a dollar.

The pitcher is an artist.

There's nothing like a ball park hot dog—and it's cheap.

Each player in baseball is an individual.

There's no time clock in baseball (unlike football, etc.)

Kids love the game.

Fenway Park is a beautiful ball park.

A home run is the only sports maneuver where the object is to *lose* the ball.

It's a game of skill, not strength.

The catcher is the unsung hero of the game.

Baseball doesn't have any secret strategies (like plays in football), so everybody can enjoy it.

If we wanted to develop a theme from these comments, we would first have to decide what subject areas are included. There are three possibilities. The first is that you can get inexpensive seats and food, and that baseball can be enjoyed by everyone, including kids. Couldn't these ideas be included as one topic—the idea of availability? Second, there are two comments about the physical place: Fenway's beauty and the organ music. Thirdly, there are comments about the unique characteristics of the game.

In what order should we put these major ideas? The most likely arrangement is to first introduce the reader to Fenway Park itself. Next, describe the advantages of baseball—its availability. Finally, present baseball's unique characteristics. In this organization, we have moved from the simplest ideas to the more complex. The following, shows how the outline might look.

I. Atmosphere
   A. Beauty of Fenway Park
   B. Organ music

II. Availability
   A. Low cost
      1. One dollar bleacher seats
      2. Inexpensive food
   B. Enjoyment of children
   C. Absence of specialized plays

III. Unique characteristics
   A. Skill preferred over strength
   B. Absence of time clock
   C. Goal of "losing" ball
   D. Individuality of each player
      1. The pitcher
      2. The catcher

The thesis statement of this theme might be: Baseball is a popular American sport because it is both available and unique.


## Preparation

As soon as you know the major headings of your paper, you can begin to prepare a rough outline. It's smart to do so, because the outline can give you other ideas. Also, it lets you see what research you have left to do. In the Baseball outline, for example, are there areas which might be further developed?

Begin by making a list of the subject headings on your note cards. Are any of them closely related or have a common theme? Perhaps they should be joined under a larger heading. Can any of them be broken down into smaller headings? For example, if you have a lot of note cards with the heading "Causes of air pollution," you may want to separately list each cause.

Now write your thesis statement, no matter how tentative, at the top of your list. Do your subject headings support your thesis statement? If they do not, is it clear that you are presenting counter evidence?

Let's say you are writing about public television. Your thesis statement is: *The economic future of public television is in danger.* You write down the following subject areas:

1. Federal cuts in spending

2. Increased competition from pay and cable television

3. Expanding audience

4. Growing production costs

5. Decreased corporate funding

6. Popularity of "Sesame Street" and "Masterpiece Theatre"

Which of these does not support the thesis statement? Obviously, numbers (3) and (6) are examples of present and future money sources since public television is publicly supported. So, they are not an economic danger and should be left out. You might begin your paper by acknowledging this positive information in the following way: "Despite the continuing popularity of such shows as *Sesame Street* and *Masterpiece Theatre,* and an ever-expanding audience, the future of public television is in danger."

In what order should we put the four major ideas that are left? It is a good idea to move from the weakest idea to the strongest, but in this case the points seem equally strong. You might begin with the immediate problem of production, move to the problem of competition, and conclude with the threats to funding, withdrawal of Federal aid being the most important. The list would now look like this:

1. Growing production costs

2. Increased competition from pay and cable television

3. Decreased corporate funding

4. Federal cuts in spending

In the next few pages, we will suggest ways to arrange an outline, but there is no hard and fast rule. You must judge for yourself if the sequence you've chosen is the most sensible one for your subject.

From rough jottings to final draft, outlines do not have to be perfect. It is in the nature of outlines to change; to adapt to new information and categories. Don't be afraid to revise frequently. Even after you begin writing, you may discover a new topic or arrangment. In this case, re-write the outline as you go along. The outline should reflect what you've done as well as what you're going to do.

Here is a common system for making an outline. Indentation shows the degree of importance.

I. _____

   A. _____

      1. _____

         a. _____

         b. _____

      2. _____

   B. _____

II. _____

## Kinds of Outlines

You may write either a topic outline or a sentence outline. A *topic outline* uses topics, not sentences. Topics are not punctuated with a period. The Baseball outline was a topic outline. A *sentence outline* expands each topic into a complete, fully punctuated sentence. Here is the Baseball outline converted to a sentence outline.

### BASEBALL

I. Baseball has a special atmosphere.
   A. Fenway Park is small but beautiful.
   B. There is live organ music.

II. Baseball is available to all.
   A. It is inexpensive.
      1. Bleacher seats are only a dollar.
      2. Hot dogs are cheap and good.
   B. Children love baseball.
   C. The absence of specialized plays means a wider audience.

III. Baseball has many unique characteristics.
   A. Skill is preferred over strength.
   B. There is no time clock, as there is in football or basketball.
   C. In the most desirable defensive play, the goal, is to "lose" the ball.
   D. The individuality of each player is very important.
      1. The pitcher is the true artist.
      2. The catcher is the unsung hero.

For some, a topic outline may be the quicker and easier form. On the other hand, a sentence outline forces you to think in complete thoughts. Your ideas are presented in fuller fashion, and you can sometimes use the sentences as topic sentences in your finished draft. (A topic sentence expresses the main idea in a paragraph.)

# Characteristics of a Good Outline

- *All parts of the outline should relate to the thesis statement.*

  Thesis statement: The language of television advertising is specialized to appeal to various audiences.

### INCORRECT

I. Prime time audiences
II. Images of children on television
III. Women (daytime)
IV. Women (prime time)
V. Radio jingles
VI. News-watching audiences

### CORRECT

I . Prime time audiences
II. Women (daytime)
III. Women (prime time)
IV. News-watching audiences

- *The outline should cover the subject.*

### INCORRECT

The Future of Private Education
I. Men's colleges
II. Co-ed schools
III. Four-year colleges

### CORRECT

The Future of Private Education
I. Men's institutions
II. Women's institutions
III. Co-ed institutions
IV. Four-year colleges
V. Universities and graduate programs

- *The outline should be in logical, appropriate sequence.* In general, you should end with your most interesting and strongest evidence. There are several ways to accomplish this.

- *Move from basic conditions to more complicated issues.*

  Adequacy of Public Health Services.
  I. Public's use
  II. Facilities
  III. Doctor's role
  IV. Government policy

- *Build an argument from weakest to strongest points.*

  Argument for Control of Handguns
  I. Handguns are easily purchased.
  II. Handguns are not used by sportsmen.
  III. Handguns figure largely in murders committed each year.

- *Move from smallest to largest or from largest to smallest.*

  Hunting Regulations
  I. Local
  II. State
  III. National

  The Painting of Edgar Degas
  I. General techniques
  II. Subject matter
  III. "The Absinthe Drinker"

- *Use chronological development.*

  The John Birch Society
  I. Founding
  II. Early history
  III. Development
  IV. The Society today

- *The headings in an outline must be coordinated:* that is, major and subordinate ideas are in their right place.

### INCORRECT

Sources of Protein
I. Animal
II. Meat
III. Fish
IV. Dried beans

### CORRECT

Sources of Protein
I. Animal
   A. Meat
   B. Fish
   C. Eggs and milk
II. Vegetables
   A. Dried beans
   B. Whole grains

- *The outline should have no single entries.*

### INCORRECT
I. Animal
   A. Meat
II. Vegetables

### CORRECT
I. Meat
II. Vegetables

- *The outline should use consistent, parallel structure.* This is especially important if you are required to submit your outline with your term paper.

### INCORRECT

Preparation of the Outline
I. Rough notes (phrase)
II. Material is organized according to major ideas. (complete sentence)
III. How to put material in proper order. (sentence fragment)
IV. Does the material support your thesis statement? (question)

---

## QUICK TEST

1. Rewrite the preceding outline, using either topic or sentence form, to make the language parallel.

2. Rewrite the following outlines, putting them in logical sequence and removing any material which does not belong. Subordinate ideas when necessary.

Causes of Air Pollution
I. Incomplete combustion of fuel
II. Chemical wastes deposited in rivers
III. Effects of air pollution
IV. Inefficient coal furnaces
V. Definition of air pollution
VI. Industrial wastes

The Work Force in the Automobile Industry
I. Productivity
II. Labor relations
III. History
IV. Present workers' conditions
V. The future of automation in the assembly line

---

# Kinds of Writing

## *Analysis*

A term paper is a composition of a special kind. It gives an analysis. When you analyze something you take it apart to understand it better. Let's look at an example of informal analysis in everyday life. This may help you understand how natural and necessary a method it is. You've just gone to see a movie, and a friend wants to know about it. First, you say, "It's playing at the Rialto; it's two hours long." But that's not what your friend wants to know. "How was it?" she asks again. This time you reply, "I cried all the way through it." Is this an analysis? No, it's a description of your feelings, not an analysis of the movie. Finally you say, "The first part really gives the feeling of coal-mining country. The actors don't look like actors; they look like poor, back-country people. The house the girl lives in looks less like a set than a real house, worn-down and shabby.

Now you have begun to provide an analysis. It is rough and informal, but it breaks down the separate elements of the movie—acting, sets, directing. This breaking-down process is important because everything is made up of smaller parts. You cannot understand the whole unless you understand its parts.

*The first step in analysis is to list the separate parts.* If you were researching different methods of delivering babies, for example, you might jot down a list something like this: doctor's attitudes, delivery room, nurses, use of anesthesia, presence of husband, post-delivery care of baby and mother, and so on.

Next ask yourself how each part works. How does anesthesia work? What happens in a delivery room? At this point you need a fundamental, not a sophisticated understanding. As you continue your research, and the process of analysis, you will learn more about parts and the way they work.

For three or four of the subjects given below, list as many separate elements as you can, and mentally define their functions.

Major league baseball

Student government

Situation comedies on television

Food stamp program

A school building, like the student union or library

---

*The second step in analysis is the discovery of relationships between parts and between parts and the whole.* When we study the Mona Lisa, for example, we want to think of the relationship between the subject matter and the *way* it's painted, and we might also consider the Mona Lisa's relationship to Leonardo's other work (was it his best painting?) or its influence on painting in general.

An analysis can be as simple as understanding the separate parts of a bicycle, or as complex as a book devoted to analyzing one work of art. Here is an example of an informal analysis.

### CITY LIFE

The pleasure of big city life lies in its many entertainments. Opera, theatre, ballet, and concerts are available every night of the week. The city dweller can hear a jazz pianist or Mozart. He can attend a musical comedy or a revival of Shakespeare. Museums offer an exhibit of Picasso's paintings or a collection of Eskimo sculpture. There are many free entertainments as well, like zoos and parks. Walkers can tour areas of special historical interest, or places that are simply fun to visit. You can discover the little-used book store, the cheap Spanish cafe, or the old-fashioned tailor. City dwellers take advantage of this diversity. After the opera, they may grab a sandwich at the nearest delicatessen. They may shop in the biggest, most glamorous stores and the smallest boutiques. In a brief walk, they go past an elegant city square and a noisy fish market. There are a hundred worlds for the city dweller to enjoy.

---

**QUICK TEST**

1. List the elements of city life found in this paragraph.

2. What is the main idea of the paragraph? Is it clearly stated?

## Comparison

When we analyze things, we sometimes use *comparisons* and *contrasts*. A comparison shows how things are similar. A contrast shows how they are different. However, since they are two sides of the same coin, we'll refer to both processes by the general term *comparison*.

A comparison is useful in several ways. First, *comparison can examine the way things work* or function. Comparing the functions of two subjects sometimes gives a clearer picture of each one. For example, comparing the House of Representatives and the Senate helps us understand better how each of them works.

The following comparisons are examples of how comparing can help explain how things work:

> propeller planes/jet planes
>
> female metabolism/male metabolism
>
> general practitioner/medical specialist

*A comparison can also show advantages or make judgments*. Before you buy a car, for example, you look at models in your price range and compare their fuel consumption, style, special features, and so on. Then you judge which car is best for you. The following are some comparisons which would help to show advantages or make judgments:

> organic gardening/chemical gardening
>
> solar energy/nuclear energy
>
> vegetable protein/animal protein
>
> renting a house/buying a house
>
> jogging/walking
>
> liberal arts education/vocational training

*Comparisons can also show change and development*. In this way, we can understand the history of something. Here are some comparisons which show change:

> urban crime: 19th century/20th century
>
> popular music: 1950s/1980s
>
> female employment: during World War II/after World War II
>
> attitudes toward Vietnam: 1964/1973
>
> fuel consumption: 1930/1980

Finally, *comparison makes us look closely at things*. It sheds light on both things being compared. It also shows how opinions can differ. Comparing opposing opinions is important in a term paper, especially when the subject is very complicated. The following comparison, from a term paper on Shakespeare's play *Henry V,* contrasts two views of the real, historical king.

> Holinshed's *Chronicles* (1587) portrays Henry V as a man everybody loved for his honor, courage, intelligence, and generosity. He ate and drank moderately; "wantonness of life and thirst of avarice" were absent in him. A good and nimble athlete, he was an expert in military matters, rarely losing a battle. Holinshed claims that Henry "both lived and died a pattern in princehood." However, William Hazlitt, in his essay of 1818, presents a quite different conception of Henry. He finds him a dissolute, idle, mischief-making fellow with no sense of right or wrong in either public or private life. In Hazlitt's view, he was a brutal robber and murderer who made war in order to secure his own shaky claims to the throne, a man "with no idea of the common decencies of life..."

There are several rules for making comparisons in a term paper. Four of them are discussed below:

*Limit the subjects for comparison.* You can't compare the entire House of Representatives with the Senate, all of World War I with World War II, or the entire history of English theatre with that of Italian theatre. The best comparisons are limited and focussed.

*Compare things in the same class, or category.* Don't compare apples with peacocks, or college life with rodeo competition. Compare apples with other foods. Compare college life with high school life.

*Make comparisons which are useful.* There is little point to comparing the weather conditions in Alaska to those in the Caribbean, or methods of extracting oil in the Sahara to ocean-floor methods. A good rule of thumb is this: The two things being compared should have a common ground, with enough differences to be interesting.

*Don't merely list similarities and differences.* If you compare the U.S. House of Representatives with the Senate, you might say that the House has two-year terms and the Senate six-year terms. But that fact alone isn't useful until you analyze its effects on Representatives or Senators: the former group must run for office every other year, while the latter has much longer between re-election. (This affects voting behavior, visits to the home state, etc.).

## Cause and Effect

*Like making comparisons, examining cause and effect is an important tool of analysis.* When you examine changes, ask yourself: What caused these changes? Who was helpful in making the changes? How were the changes made? For example, what has caused the upswing in crime in the cities during the last hundred years? Why did the female work force diminish during the 1950s? What are the causes of increased lung cancer in the U.S.?

Note: Keep in mind that you're looking for *strong probable causes*. In discussing changing attitudes toward the Vietnam War, for example, it may be better to ask yourself: What influenced changing opinion? You can make a very good case for probable influences without having to explain *all* possible causes.

Now, let's look at effects, or consequences. Ask yourself: *What* were the effects? *Who* was affected? *How* were people, institutions, laws, behavior, ideas, etc. affected? What were the consequences of fewer working women in the 1950s? Does the public's changed view on the Vietnam war affect attitudes toward veterans?

Be careful about determining causes and effects. Don't be too hasty about linking up the Women's Movement with an increase in the divorce rate, or in connecting eating yogurt with longer life. In a term paper, you must provide solid evidence to support your claim. The following paragraph sets forth one of the causes of inflation.

### A CAUSE OF INFLATION

Although prices can rise for many reasons—for example a new make of car may have a lot of improvements and therefore cost more than the old model—inflation happens when prices rise and there have not been any improvements in the products you buy. Many things can cause inflation. One of the most important causes is that industry has to pay more to produce the same product without making it any better. Costs can increase because a labor contract has increased the wages of the worker who makes the product. The price of oil required to generate energy to run the machines that make the product can go up. Interest rates charged to the producer to borrow money can go up. All these cost increases get passed along to the consumer who is getting the same product at a higher price. The consumer then demands that his wages be increased to meet the higher prices, and an inflationary cycle begins.

---

## QUESTIONS

1. What is the central idea of the paragraph?

2. What elements does this paragraph set forth as causing inflation? How do they relate to the central idea?

---

Making an analysis by finding comparisons or by examining causes or effects is useful in several ways. First, using them helps you train your mind to think analytically. Second, they are excellent ways to organize a term paper. They give you, the writer, a clear structure to build on and they give the reader a clear structure to follow.

Prepare a brief paragraph on one or more of the following:

An analysis of the grading system

A comparison between home economics and shop as vocational courses

A comparison of two magazine advertisements: one directed at women, the other at men

An examination of the possible causes of holiday depression

A look at the effects of daily exercise

## Argument

Persuasion, or argument, is a careful analysis intended to persuade the reader to share the writer's viewpoint. When you present the evidence in an argument, you do so in order to persuade your reader to accept your conclusions. In a sense, all term papers are arguments. You are arguing that your thesis statement, your evidence, and your conclusions are valid.

There may be a reasonable disagreement between informed people. Therefore, you must respect your reader by giving the best evidence you can. Do not begin with a prejudice. You will only be looking for material to support that prejudice. Do not dismiss any important evidence even if it is in disagreement with you. Try to see the issues with objectivity.

Sometimes your argument may be only part of your paper, perhaps the final paragraph. For example, if you are writing on the social effects of alcoholism, you may wish to conclude with a brief argument for better diagnosis and treatment of the disease.

Choose to present that evidence in the form of an argument paper. That is certainly the best way to write an argument term paper—to begin with an open mind.

Perhaps you are writing a paper called "The Case for Solar Energy." You will begin by presenting the case *against* solar energy and you will do so fairly. Do not hedge by trying to weaken the evidence. Even though this section of your paper may be brief, it should fully cover the opposing evidence. Then you will proceed to the arguments *for* solar energy. You will build to your strongest or most complex argument.

Sometimes your argument may be only part of your paper, perhaps the final paragraph. For example, if you are writing on the social effects of alcoholism, you may wish to conclude with a brief argument for better diagnosis of the disease.

The following is an example of an argument in the form of a brief essay.

## COMPULSORY NATIONAL SERVICE

The draft was ended in the United States at the end of the Vietnam War because large numbers of people, especially young people, opposed it. They opposed it in part because it was unfair. The more privileged a young man's background the smaller the chances he would have to serve. But the time has come to reinstate the draft in the form of compulsory national service for all Americans.

In order to attract recruits, the army must pay competitive wages. People join up to learn a skill and when they have learned it, they leave the army for jobs with higher salaries. The army must bear the cost of continually retraining new personnel. Furthermore, people who do join today's army are from less privileged backgrounds; so the old problem is still there.

A fair draft would require every American to spend a year or two after high school in national service. A lottery would determine which would serve in the army and which in public service jobs. Those jobs might be such much-needed work as cleaning up our cities, maintaining public lands, and working for public agencies which were short of manpower. Compulsory national service would restore a sense of morale and achievement to young adults and develop a spirit of patriotism and commitment which they'd take with them into private life.

---

**QUICK TEST**

1. How does this essay deal with the opposing view?

2. What is the central idea of the essay?

3. Does the essay leave out important reasons for opposing the draft?

4. What arguments could you give for keeping a volunteer army?

---

## Other Kinds of Writing

In your term paper, you may utilize one of the following kinds of writing: exposition, definition, narration, description.

*Exposition.* Coming from the Latin word *exponere,* "to put forth," exposition sets forth information, gives explanations or reveals a process. It is the most common kind of writing. Examples of exposition are: directions for making an omelet, directions for filling out a form, a statement of purpose of an organization, an explanation of how smoking affects your heart.

Here is an example of exposition from a term paper on ancient India.

### THE WIDOW

When a woman's husband died, she also became "dead" to society. She shaved her head, ate only one meal a day without any spices, slept on the ground, and gave up personal adornment of any kind. She was regarded as a sign of bad luck, and was not welcome at family parties. She was even shunned by servants. Her days were spent praying for her husband's soul. Given this unhappy life, it's no wonder that many widows chose to immolate themselves on their husbands' funeral pyres.

*Definition.* Definitions can range in length from a short dictionary description of a word to entire books devoted to defining one concept. In a term paper, it is necessary to define (1) your central term and important supporting words, and (2) any technical or difficult words whose meaning would be unclear to your reader. It is better to have too many definitions than not enough.

For example, near the beginning of this book we provide a definition of the term paper. If you are writing on the Iroquois Indians, you'll want to give a definition of that tribe. If your term paper is on social interaction in public places, you must define the phrase "social interaction." Defining a central term will probably require at least a paragraph. Here for example is a definition from a term paper on the artist Degas.

### IMPRESSIONISM

Impressionism, which flourished in France in the 1870's, was a rebellion against formal art. It brought painting out of the studio and into the open air. Impressionists wanted each painting to represent an actual moment, unlike the carefully posed academic paintings. They were interested in the interplay of light and color, painting with a small stroke of bright color, which resulted in a lack of modeling or outline. Thus, Impressionist paintings often seem to be shimmering in light.

For central definitions of this kind, it isn't good enough merely to quote the dictionary. You must show your readers that you have absorbed and understood enough information about the concept to explain it.

If you are not defining a term which is central to your paper, you may only need a brief definition:

Cezanne was later identified with Post-Impressionism, a reaction against Impressionism which stressed a return to subject matter and underlying form.

*Narration.* A narration gives an account of events as they happened in time. History, biography, and autobiography are all narrations. You will use narrative elements when you need to fill in historical background. For example, you might give a summary of events leading up to the Battle of Gettysburg.

You might provide a brief history of the uses of solar power. You will use biography to introduce an important character and let us know something about him. The following is an example of narration.

## JOSEPH CONRAD

Joseph Conrad was born in Poland in 1857. Son of aristocratic parents, he went to sea at the age of sixteen. A few years later he entered the British merchant service and later became a British citizen. His life at sea gave him the material for many of his novels. He left the sea at the age of 32, married, and began writing. Although Polish was his native tongue and he didn't learn English until he was 20, he ultimately became one of the greatest English novelists. *Lord Jim* (1900) and *Youth* (1902) are among his widely-acclaimed works. He died in England in 1924.

## QUESTION

When would it be useful to introduce a biographical note such as this?

*Description.* A description gives a sensory impression of a person, place, object, or feeling. By sensory we mean having to do with the five sense, often that of sight. Descriptions are welcome in a term paper, where they can make writing more vivid and provide a pleasant change in tone. Read the following example.

## PARKFAIRFAX

Parkfairfax in Alexandria, Virginia is a rental community of over 1,600 apartments. Its red-brick townhouses are modest and lack ornament. Wide grassy areas are worn in spots and threaded with scraggly footpaths. Some of the spaces between the buildings are filled with trees and bushy undergrowth. Vegetable and flower gardens grow in available space, and some residents have terraced the land next to their doors. Cats, though forbidden, moon in the windows. Nothing whatever happens here. This pleasant, backwater atmosphere is soon to come to an end, however. International Developers, Inc. have just forked over $30 million in order to convert Parkfairfax to condominiums.

## QUESTIONS

1.  What are the most important words the author uses to describe Parkfairfax? What is the effect of the adjectives chosen?

2.  This is the first paragraph of an essay describing radical changes proposed for the rental community. What is the purpose of this description?

**EXERCISES**

1. Write a biographical sketch of one of your favorite grandparents.

2. Describe some well-known public building in your town (for example, a church, courthouse, historical building).

3. Give your own definition of one of the following terms: high fashion, terrorism, junk food, horror movie, rock and roll.

4. Explain a process you understand well. For example: changing a tire, making bread, running a mile, planting a garden, sailing a boat, sewing a button on a coat.

## The Literary Term Paper

If you are writing a term paper on a genre of literature — poem, play, novel, short story, etc. — begin by coming to a solid understanding of the work before reading criticism. Make sure, first of all, that you can explain the basic situation of the work. Be able to answer for yourself such questions as: "Who is speaking? What is happening? Who are the characters? What is their relationship to one another? What do all the words mean? Next decide for yourself the meaning of the work. Ask yourself: What is the theme? What are the images or symbols? What kind of language is used? Each work of art will produce a different set of questions.

At this point, you may want to write down some of your thoughts, either as a list of ideas, a rough outline or rough notes. These notes will be your focus as you do your research.

You must now find sources that support (and deny) your claims. Therefore, the process is something like watching a tennis match: you examine the literary work, then the source materials, then the work again. Then you try to link the two.

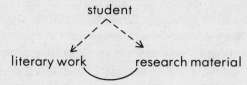

The following are some suggestions for literary analysis:

- _Look for repetitions._ Repeated images, words, and actions are sometimes clues to meaning.

- _Look for contrasts_. It may be helpful to examine contrasts between characters, values, actions, images, old and new, good and evil, the past and the present.

- _Read for detail._ It may not be accurate to say "every word counts," but in most well-constructed works it is safe to say nothing is accidental.

# Writing the Paper

## *Supporting Your Ideas*

Now you are ready to write. You have before you your thesis statement and your outline. Your note cards are roughly arranged according to the major and minor headings of the outline. Glance through the materials again to make sure you're familiar with them.

Your basic task is to support each of the ideas in your outline. To do this, you must: be specific, be concrete, and support generalizations with examples.

*Be specific.* This is a good rule for all writing. Specific words are precise and definite. General words are vague and less limited in scope. Specifics are strong, helping us understand by example.

GENERAL: He is an unjust ruler.

SPECIFIC: He has plundered our seas, ravaged our coasts, burnt our towns, and destroyed the lives of our people.
—The Declaration of Independence

GENERAL: Everyone knows the divorce rate is rising.

SPECIFIC: Americans obtained divorces in 1979 at more than twice the rate they did twenty years earlier, according to a new Government study.

One of the best ways to be specific is to *be concrete*. Use concrete words to support abstract ideas. An abstract word expresses ideas, theories, and concepts. It's important to think abstractly; it's also important for the writer to present concrete examples. Concrete words refer to particular things, to things which can be seen, touched, tasted, felt, heard.

GENERAL AND ABSTRACT: Thoreau was dressed as a naturalist.

CONCRETE AND SPECIFIC: Under his arm he carried an old music-book to press plants; in his pocket were his diary and pencil, a spy-glass for birds, microscope, jack-knife and twine. He wore a straw hat, stout shoes, strong gray trousers. . . to climb a tree for a hawk's or a squirrel's nest.

—Ralph Waldo Emerson

GENERAL AND ABSTRACT: The white birch has many uses for man.

CONCRETE AND SPECIFIC: Birch bark has been used for canoes, boxes, cups, lampshades, furniture, and painting surfaces. The lumber has been made into bowls and dishes and used as fuel. The leaves of the birch can be steeped for tea.

*Support all generalizations with specific examples.* Remember your interested reader with a need to know: he or she needs examples and illustrations. Be generous in giving them. Don't be miserly with the evidence—the facts, statistics, information, specifics—which you have acquired through research.

GENERALIZATION: There is new evidence of lower achievement in school.

SUPPORTED WITH SPECIFICS: A report shows that the reasoning ability of 13-year olds and 17-year olds has declined, as measured by their ability to draw conclusions, form judgments and create new ideas.

GENERALIZATION: The governor announced that the strike has had devasting economic effects.

SUPPORTED WITH SPECIFICS: The state is losing $500,000 in tax revenues, a total of $48 billion a month. State spending has been cut ten per cent, and the legislature is considering emergency appropriations to keep schools open.

GENERALIZATION: The traditional American family is changing.

SUPPORTED WITH SPECIFICS: The definition of a typical American family as a husband, non-working wife, and two children is changing. Under half of all families consist of a husband and wife in a first marriage. Almost 50 per cent of children under eighteen will live at one time with a single parent. Nearly 60 per cent of wives are in the work force.

## QUICK TEST

Examine the following generalizations. What examples can you find to support each one? Be as specific as you can.

1. Television game shows appeal to certain basic desires.

2. Competitive sports require many skills.

3. A college education is expensive.

4. City slums are ugly.

5. Traveling is a useful experience.

6. Movies increasingly portray the violent aspect of life.

## Paragraphs

*What* you write must be as specific and concrete as possible. *How* you write is also important. The basic unit of writing is the paragraph; it allows us to express thoughts in a manageable form. In addition, it is a necessary convenience for the reader: we read by paragraphs.

A paragraph can take a variety of shapes. It may be short or long. It may contrast two things. It may list a series of things (as we are doing here). It may introduce an idea or present a conclusion. It may analyze, describe, define, narrate, explain or argue. Whatever its purpose, a good paragraph has two characteristics. First, it is unified. Second, the sentences within it flow naturally one to the next.

A paragraph is unified if each sentence in it contributes to a central idea. This central idea is almost always stated in a *topic sentence*. The topic sentence often appears as the first sentence of the paragraph; less often, it appears at the end. Don't hide the topic sentence in the middle of the paragraph. Be sure each sentence in the paragraph relates to the topic sentence.

Sentences flow readably within the paragraph when the meaning between them is clear. *The relationship between ideas in sentences should be clearly expressed.* This is one of the most important rules in writing.

> WEAK: I like jazz. I like Mozart.

> REVISED: I like jazz. I also like the music of Mozart.

> WEAK: It rained for two days. The reservoir is full.

> REVISED: It rained for two days. As a result, the reservoir is full.

> WEAK: I took a long walk. I laid down.

> REVISED: I took a long walk. Then, I lay down to rest for a while.

As you can see, the meaning is clarified and strengthened in the revised sentences. This clarification is achieved through the means of *transition words*. Use transitions to clearly relate each sentence to the one before it. There are a number of transitional devices which are useful.

*Pronouns*
Professor Jackson is in Africa. *He* is doing research there.
John and Jill started a weekly newspaper. Now, *they* are going bankrupt.

*Repeat words and phrases*
Crowds gained a new perspective at the *Picasso* exhibit this summer. For the first time, *Picasso's* work has been presented properly.

*Use synonyms or closely related words*
Eight per cent of the country is *out of work*. The highest rate of *unemployment* is in the cities.
There was no *motive* for the mayor's disappearance. Most *reasons* seemed implausible.
*Money* talks. There's nothing like hard *cash* to convince a man.

You can also use transitional words and phrases to achieve the following:

*Amplify what you've said*
And, moreover, further, furthermore, in addition, besides, also, too

*Make comparisons and contrasts*
Likewise, similarly, but, yet, however, nevertheless, still, on the other hand, in contrast

*Enumerate*
First, second, next, in the first place, first of all, finally, last

*Express time*
To begin, at first, soon, then, meanwhile, afterward, last

*Make examples*
For example, for instance, to illustrate

*Intensify a point*
Indeed, of course, clearly, in fact

*Reach conclusions*
Therefore, so, as a result, as a consequence, consequently, thus

*Summarize*
In other words, to sum up, in brief, in short, to summarize

In the two paragraphs below, the transitional devices have been underlined. What is the central idea of each paragraph? Is it expressed in a topic sentence? Are generalizations supported by specific examples?

The Elizabethans ate and drank extravagantly. *First of all, they* had a natural talent for *drunkenness,* "the heavy-headed revel" as Hamlet puts it. *They* began the day, *for example,* by *drinking* beer and went on to greater *consumption* and stronger spirits. *In addition, they put away great* quantities of food. Here are the *foods* served at one banquet in 1605: roast beef, salted beef, veal, mutton, turkey, capon, boiled hen, partridge, larks, quails, snipe, woodcock, salmon, sole, lobster, rabbits, artichokes, turnips, peas, cheese, and quince pie. The *food* was so abundant that servants were fed on the leftovers. *Clearly*, appetite was the genius of the age.

In the set designer's office, there were none of the props one usually associates with the theatre. *There were no* old posters, playbills, or autographed photographs. *There were no* scraps of fabric or torn furls of colored paper. *There was no* rich smell of glue and paint. *On the contrary*, everything was spare and bright. The furniture was all chrome and *clean* white plastic. The floors were *bare* of litter. *This* high-tech order and *cleanliness* was appropriate, *however;* the set designer worked for a television studio.

---

## QUICK TEST

In the following two paragraphs, underline the transitional devices and identify the central idea of the paragraph.

Members of a Congressional staff are often more insecure and cautious than their bosses. Staffers are not protected by bureaucratic regulations or by a civil service. Therefore they owe their continued employment to the good will of their Congressman. To secure that good will, staffers tend not to take independent action. The price of such action—for example, advising the Congressman to take a strong stand on a controversial issue like busing—is often to be suddenly out of work. To protect their jobs, therefore, staffers often give up their political autonomy. As a result, a bold and decisive legislator may be supported by a timid, unimaginative staff.

I rejoice that there are owls. Let them do the idiotic and maniacal hooting for men. It is a sound admirably suited to swamps and twilight woods which no day illuminates, suggesting a vast and undeveloped nature which men have not recognized. Owls represent the stark twilight and unsatisfied thoughts which all have. All day the sun has shone on the surface of the some savage swamp, where the small hawks circulate above. But now a more dismal and fitting day dawns. A different race of creatures awakes to express the meaning of nature there.

—adapted from Henry David Thoreau

---

Clarify the meaning in the following sentences by providing transitional expressions.

1. Literature is filled with characters and stories. Music is abstract.

2. The construction of the Panama Canal had many setbacks. The mosquito caused widespread yellow fever.

3. Mortgage rates are going up. Fewer people than ever can afford to own their own homes.

4. Hemingway's novels are terse. His letters are talky and almost long-winded.

5. The stock market collapsed in 1929. America entered into a period of economic depression.

6. Writing a term paper teaches the student how to do library research. It teaches organizational and writing skills.

7. George Washington was a solid and competent leader. Thomas Jefferson was an inventor and a man of many talents.

8. Check the card catalog in your subject area. Consult pertinent reference works. Ask the librarian for advice.

Transitions between paragraphs are as important as transitions between sentences, and use the same transitional devices. In a new paragraph, ask yourself if you are continuing the same train of thought. If so, write "in addition" or "moreover" in the first sentence. Are you suggesting a turn or contrast? Write "in contrast" or "on the other hand." Are you summarizing or reaching a conclusion? Write "finally" or "to sum up" or therefore." Remember, *the first sentence of each paragraph should contain a transitional expression relating it to the paragraph before it*

## QUICK TEST

Take a look at the editorial page of a major daily newspaper. Without reading for content, make a list of the transitional expressions used in the first sentence of each paragraph. You will find that in most instances, the writers make clear references to a transition in thought. Now, read the editorials and you'll see how the writers use repetition, synonyms, and closely related words to provide a logical flow between and within paragraphs.

## Writing Clearly

The most effective and successful writing is simple, direct, and uncluttered. Unfortunately, we hear cluttered and unclear language around us all the time.

The weatherman says "precipitation" when he means rain or snow. A politician says, "I'll be factoring in the various possibilities and coming to a tentative conclusion" instead of saying, "maybe." An educator writes "dysfunctional learning ability and absence of motivational goals" to describe a student who is having problems with schoolwork. The Federal government installs a slideshow in Washington, DC, Union Station, and calls it a "Primary Audio Visual Experience." When authorities use such overblown language, it's easy to assume that it is the correct form of expression. It isn't.

Simple writing, however, does not mean simple-minded thinking. Subtle and complex ideas may be expressed in very simple sentences. In fact, difficult, complex thoughts *need* clear expression. For example:

> The electron is a small particle bearing a charge of negative electricity.

This is a complex idea, but there is nothing unnecessary in its expression. Compare it to the following:

> The electron is a piece of matter, extremely little in size, which transports a quantity of negatively-charged electricity.

Nothing has been added but words. Following are some rules regarding clear writing.

- *Be concise*. Do not use unnecessary words. If a word has no function in the sentence, take it out.

> Ask not what your country can do for you—ask what you can do for your country.

This famous statement uses eight common words, seven of which are in one syllable. It is powerful because it is brief and concise.

Read the following examples of wordy and concise statements.

> WORDY: In today's contemporary society, women are beginning to perceive that they are being paid inadequately and they are asking that this situation be changed.

Doesn't contemporary mean the same thing as today? Do any women exist outside of society? How does "beginning to perceive" differ from actually perceiving? We use phrases like this without thinking. Here is the revision.

> REVISED: Women want equal pay for equal work.

Often the introductory phrases "there is" or "there are" are necessary, but often they are merely extra words and don't add to the meaning of the sentence.

WORDY: There are many counselors who are presently advising retirees to pursue leisure-time activities.

REVISED: Many counselors advise retired men and women to get interested in a hobby.

WORDY: There are eight million inhabitants of New York.

REVISED: Eight million people live in New York.

Following, are some additional examples of wordiness.

WORDY: We are meeting together today on an important field of battle of that armed conflict.

REVISED: We are met in a great battlefield of that war.
—Abraham Lincoln

WORDY: The desire to draw is as inborn an impulse as the desire to express oneself through speech.

REVISED: The impulse to draw is as natural as the impulse to talk.

- *Avoid qualifiers and qualifications.* Make positive assertions whenever possible. Don't dilute your ideas by constantly using words like *rather, perhaps, sometimes, somewhat, seems, a little, kind of*. Even intensifying words like *very* and *really* can weaken your point through overstatement. Decide what you mean and say it. Don't hedge by using these little words to moderate and soften your meaning.

WEAK: The welfare system is somewhat in need of reform.

REVISED: The welfare system is in need of reform.

WEAK: Picasso was kind of a genius.

REVISED: Picasso was a genius.

WEAK: It was rather nice to walk with him.

REVISED: It was a pleasure to walk with him.

---

## QUICK TEST

Revise the following sentences to eliminate wordiness and weak qualifiers.

1. Thousands of years ago, the Ancient Greeks were the first to come to the conclusion that the planet earth was spherical in shape.

2. One reason we have decided to adopt the metric system is because of the fact that the rest of the world is using it.

3. There is a new book recently issued that collects Flaubert's letters.

4. In August, the plains are brown in hue.

5. Graham Greene's novels were rather influenced by the thriller movie.

6. At some distant time in the future, on account of rapid technological development, we may be able to vacation on Mars.

7. In a band, you may have many different kinds of musical instruments.

8. Insects are a pretty big class of invertebrate animals.

9. It is estimated that about one in twenty-five of all human beings who have ever lived are alive today.

10. There is an imaginary zone of the sky over which the principal planets travel called the Zodiac.

---

- *Understand denotation and connotation.* All words have an exact, dictionary definition, or denotation. They also have a connotation, or connotative meaning, which is made up of the associations and suggestions they carry. In the sentence below, Mark Twain plays on the different connotations of three words closely related in meaning.

  The humorous story is American, the comic story is English, the witty story is French.   –Mark Twain

If you become aware of connotations, then you'll understand the political, and social colorings of many words. Look at the following list of words and phrases. What is the connotation, or associated meaning, of each word or phrase? Can you find a better, more neutral term to substitute for each word?

| | |
|---|---|
| Iron Curtain country | women's libber |
| spinster | redneck |
| Red China | flatfoot |
| Wetbacks | brainwash |
| backward nation | hordes of foreigners |

---

## QUICK TEST

Determine the connotative differences in the following groups of words:

1. rascal/villain
2. continue/persist/endure
3. steal/rob/pilfer
4. catty/feline
5. illiterate/ignorant
6. fat/chubby/obese
7. marriage/wedlock/union
8. curious/inquisitive/prying

---

## Using a Dictionary to Improve Vocabulary

Increasing your vocabulary is a good way to write with more exactness and clarity. The purpose of learning new words is not merely to accumulate them. It is to provide you with suitable words, thus enabling you to be more precise when you speak and write. The wider your range of language, the less wordy you will have to be.

Writing a term paper gives you an excellent chance to add to your vocabulary. In the course of your research, you may come across many new words which you'll need to understand and use in your writing.

Sometimes students are advised to try to figure out a word's meaning from its context before looking it up in a dictionary. We suggest, however, using a dictionary for any important word whose meaning isn't clear to you. This is a quick and efficient way to learn all of a word's meanings (there may be more than one), its pronunciation, origin, and usage. In addition, the dictionary is an excellent resource tool. It frequently provides plural forms, synonyms, use of the word in a phrase, cross references, connotations of closely related words, as well as illustrations and maps. Take a few minutes to leaf through your dictionary, making certain you understand its abbreviations, symbols, and guidelines. Then, *when you read a new word, reach for your dictionary immediately.* Let an unfamiliar word be a "stopper," stopping your eye in mid-sentence. Don't skip over it. Don't even read to the end of the paragraph before pulling out your dictionary.

Keep a paperback dictionary with you when you're studying away from your own desk; take it with you even to the library where the reference dictionaries may be several floors away. The trick is not to view using the dictionary as an interruption of your research, but as part of its natural flow.

When looking up a word, first check its pronunciation. Say the word clearly to yourself. Notice the way the word breaks down into syllables. This will help you both to pronounce and spell the word. Now, note the meanings of the word, listed by part-of-speech (noun, adjective, etc.). Decide which meaning is appropriate to your reading. Finally, read the word's *etymology*—its origin and how it developed. The etymology is usually given in brackets following the part of speech label. Knowing the word's origin will help fix the word's meaning in your mind. For example, if you look up the word *orthodox,* an adjective meaning correct and proper, you will find it comes from the Greek words *orthos,* correct + *doxa,* opinion. The original words are a kind of definition in themselves.

Here is a sample dictionary entry:

> lunatic (loo´ ne-tik, lú´ ne-tik), adj. ME. *lunatik;* OFr.; LL. *lunaticus* L. *luna,* the moon. 1. suffering from lunacy; insane. 2. of or characterized by lunacy. 3. of or for insane persons. 4. utterly foolish. n. an insane person.

From this entry, we learn that *lunatic* is a word of three syllables, and two pronunciations (the first is the preferred or more common), with the accent in each case on the first syllable. The earliest derivation of the word is from the Latin word meaning moon. It has gone through later changes in Late Latin, Old French, and Middle English. There are four meanings for the adjective form, and one for the noun.

Keep an informal list of the new words you come across; the inside cover of your notebook is a good place for such a list. At the end of your note-taking phase, re-read the words and make sure you still understand their meanings. If you really want to build your vocabulary, keep your eyes open for new words in newspapers, novels, textbooks, whenever you read.

---

**TEACH YOURSELF**

1. Learn more about word origins by looking up the etymologies of the following words: lunch, barbarous, curmudgeon, flirt, rhubarb, starling, boudoir, club, salary, gallows.

2. What do you associate with the words *graveyard* and *cemetery?* Although they are virtual synonyms, the origin of each word gives it special associations. Look up the etymology of each one.

3. When words share a common origin, they are *cognates.* Cognate comes from the Latin word meaning to be related at birth. Cognate words are cousins of each other. It's interesting to examine groups of cognates and see what different words have in common with each other. The dictionary sometimes refers you to cognates, or related words, in the etymology section of the entry. For example, under *college* you will find "see COLLEAGUE." Look up the etymologies in the following cognate group:

    a. gold, gleam, glass, glad, yellow

    b. corn, grain, kernel, churl

    c. wind, weather, ventilate

---

## *Beginnings and Endings*

If you have trouble writing the introduction to your paper, try writing it and the conclusion after you have written the body of your paper. Then you will understand exactly what you are introducing, and you'll know what points to make in your conclusion.

The introduction and conclusion function for the reader as transitions into and out of your paper. *They should be brief and to the point.* Avoid making such sweeping generalizations as: "Ever since the dawn of time..." or "Men's clothing always has, and always will..." Use the same language you have used in the rest of your paper—direct and to the point.

There is only one general rule which you should follow in writing the introduction: *Declare your thesis statement.* You don't need to do this in the very first sentence, but be sure the thesis statement is clearly stated in the first or second paragraph.

Use common sense in writing the introduction. Clearly introduce your subject. Define all important terms. Place your subject firmly in time and space. Use quotes, descriptions, examples — but only if they are clearly related to the subject and help the reader's understanding.

On the other hand the chief function of a concluding paragraph is psychological: it is awkward for the reader to come to an abrupt stop. A conclusion signals to the reader that you have completed your task. If your paper has contained complicated ideas, you may take this opportunity to summarize the main points. Or, you may briefly discuss aspects — solutions, causes, effects, future possibilities — not contained in your paper. As in the introduction, the conclusion is no place for wide-ranging speculation. A brief conclusion is better than a long-winded one.

## Revision

Revision is an essential part of writing. It is not an exercise merely tacked on at the end of your work. When you revise, you examine the major premises of your paper. Have you made each point clearly and well? Have you supported each point with evidence and examples? Have you been as specific and concrete as possible so that your reader will accept your generalizations?

Examine each sentence in your draft. Does each word convey the exact meaning you want? Are there dead words which can be cut? Lop off the wordy undergrowth, and you will begin to see your ideas really take shape.

Does the meaning flow from sentence to sentence and from paragraph to paragraph? Now is the time to insert transitions if you have not already done so. (Some writers always leave this job for the revision phase.) Ask yourself: what is the relation in meaning between one sentence and the next? Make sure it is clearly expressed.

## Revisor's Checklist

1.  Never begin with an apology: "I've researched this subject for weeks and it is still a mystery..." or "Even after reading this poem ten times, I cannot be sure of its theme..." It makes the reader uneasy to read a declaration of failure at the outset of the paper.

2.  Avoid the use of "I." This is not a hard-and-fast rule, but it may prove useful. Too many "I's" clutter up the page. Often the personal pronoun simply isn't necessary, as in the following case:

    I feel that childbirth without drugs is better for both mother and child.

    The reader knows that this is your opinion, supported by evidence. "I feel" is unnecessary; also, "feel" is an inappropriate word. The reader isn't interested in the writer's feelings. A good general rule is: Don't draw attention to yourself.

3. Use the present tense when referring to all events in a work of literature:

   NOT: Othello killed Desdemona.
   BUT: Othello kills Desdemona.

4. Do not introduce a term paper with the phrase, "According to the dictionary..." It is an overworked cliche.

5. Use standard English. A term paper should not contain slang. Substitute "children" for "kids" and "examination" for "exam."

6. Do not shift the person of the subject constantly. In the following excerpt, the writer uses four persons.

   At first, *you* may find research difficult. But as *one* proceeds, library work grows easier. The *student* who makes an effort will be rewarded. In the end, *I* acquired much useful knowledge.

# The Completed Paper

## *Acknowledging Sources*

In a term paper, you must indicate, by footnoting, whenever you have used someone else's ideas and words. Failure to acknowledge your sources is plagiarism—theft, in short.

Let's say you are writing a paper on the effects of the rising divorce rate in America. You run across a comment by journalist Ellen Goodman on post-divorce reactions: "Women mourn; men replace." Following are two ways you can handle Goodman's words and idea.

> DIRECT QUOTE: As Ellen Goodman has written, "Women mourn; men replace."

> PARAPHRASE: Ellen Goodman believes that after divorce or death women are more apt to grieve over their loss, while men hurry to find a replacement.

You *cannot* present the idea as your own, even if you use your own words and assemble your own evidence to support it.

Place the footnote at the end of the sentence containing the borrowed citation. Do not wait until the end of the paragraph.

> Ellen Goodman believes that, after divorce or death, women are more apt to grieve over their loss, while men hurry to find a replacement.[1] A recent study supports this idea: men tend to remarry at a faster rate than women, beating them to the altar by fourteen months.[2]

## *Introducing Quoted Material*

1. Short quotations are incorporated into the body of the paper. Reproduce all punctuation, spelling, and capitalization exactly as it appears in the original. Use single quotation marks for a quotation within a quotation.

   Harry S. Truman observed that the President must sometimes say to Congress "firmly and flatly, 'No, you can't do it.'"

   It is spring, that time of year when, as Chaucer wrote, "smale foweles maken melodye."

2. Follow the general rules for punctuation when quoting. If a mark of punctuation falls *outside* your quotation, omit it.

   ORIGINAL: "To read Wilbur is to experience a tremendous delight in his precision, his unfailing decorum, his cleverness, and the subtle play of his mind."

   —Donald Hall, "The New Poetry"

   QUOTATION: Donald Hall refers to the "precision" in Richard Wilbur's poetry.

   Here the comma following the quote is properly omitted.

3. Commas and periods go inside the quotation marks. Semi-colons and colons go outside.

   John F. Kennedy spoke of a loss of "moral strength"; he called for a "new generation of leadership."

4. Question marks and exclamation points go inside if they are part of the quotation, and outside if they are your punctuation.

   Ariel asks, "Do you love me, master?" What is Prospero's reply to his "delicate Ariel"?

5. Indicate omissions *within* the quotation by an ellipsis. An ellipsis is three spaced periods. When an omission occurs at the end of a sentence, add a fourth period as the terminal punctuation.

   About Abraham Lincoln, the poet commented: "Lincoln seems... the most interesting man who ever lived. He was gentle, but his gentleness was combined with a terrific toughness...."

6. Precede the quotation with a comma or colon in cases like the following. Always capitalize the first word following a colon, even if it isn't capitalized in the original.

   The novel begins with language appropriate to an epic: "It was the best of times; it was the worst of times."

   During World War II, the British novelist Virginia Woolf wrote, "we live without a future."

7. If the quoted material is an integral part of the sentence or is introduced by *that, who, which,* etc., no preceding punctuation is needed. Do not capitalize the first word even if it is capitalized in the original.

> In *Great Expectations,* Dickens notes that "in the little world in which children have their existence, whosoever brings them up, there is nothing so finely perceived and so finely felt, as injustice."

8. Set off quotations of more than four typewritten lines in single spacing, four spaces from the left margin. Double-space between the text and the quotation. If you are quoting a whole paragraph, indent four spaces for the first line. Quotation marks are not necessary in this case.

> Charles Dickens begins *David Copperfield* with these words:
>
> Whether I shall turn out to be a hero of my own life, or whether that station will be held by anybody else, these pages must show. To begin my life with the beginning of my life, I record that I was born (as I have been informed and believe) on a Friday, at twelve o'clock at night.

9. Quote poetry in one of two ways. A short quotation of two or three lines is incorporated into the text, a slash indicating the end of the line.

> In *The Rape of the Lock,* Belinda may "Forget her prayers, or miss a masquerade;/Or lose her heart, or necklace, at a ball . . ."

Longer poetry quotations are single-spaced and centered in the middle of the page. The poem's line divisions, punctuation and spelling appear as in the original.

> Nothing so true as what you once let fall,
> "Most Women have no Characters at all."
> Matter too soft a lasting mark to bear,
> And best distinguished by black, brown, or fair.
> —Alexander Pope, *Moral Essay II*

10. In a term paper frequently citing one work, give the first footnote to specify the edition you are using and explain that subsequent references to that work will be from that edition. In a parenthesis following the quotation, give the page number.

When quoting from a play, give the act, scene, and line. Put the final punctuation after the parenthesis.

> Jane Austin wryly remarks that the hero of her novel could be the model for "the hero of a favorite story" (p. 67).

> In *Henry V,* the king claims: "What infinite heart'sease/must kings neglect that private men enjoy" (IV.i. 241-42).

11. Identify the authors you are citing in the text of your paper. In other words, introduce your sources formally (a footnote is not an introduction).

> WEAK: As the essayist once remarked, "It is easier to plan a good world than a good nation..."

> REVISED: As E.B. White once wrote, "It is easier to plan..."

12. Let your reader know what you have learned about sources. Tell the reader if a source is highly qualified or biased, or has special qualifications of some kind. You don't need to do this with each source. Do so when the information being cited is highly technical or specialized, or if it is complex or controversial.

> WEAK: Dr. James Thompson believes that there is a direct correlation between lung cancer and smoking.

> REVISED: Dr. James Thompson, a senior pathologist at the Davidson Medical Center, has run three thousand tests over the past two years trying to determine a cause for lung cancer. He believes that...

## Footnotes

1. If footnotes appear at the bottom of each page, separate them from the text with one space and a typed line. Begin the footnotes one space under that.

2. Indent the first line of the footnote by five spaces.

3. Place the footnote number slightly above the line, usually one-half spacing on most typewriters. Follow with one space.

4. Single-space all footnotes. Double space *between* footnotes.

5. For the first footnote reference, give the name of the author or editor, with his first name first, followed by the title in italics (underlined), the publication data for books in parenthesis, and the page cited.

6. Use commas between each main item, and after the parenthesis.

7. End footnotes with a period.

8. For subsequent footnote references to a previously cited work, give the author's name and the page cited.

## Bibliography

Your final bibliography usually reflects the sources actually used to research the term paper. However, some teachers may ask you to include all the works you examined even if you did not cite them in a footnote.

After you have typed the paper, see which sources you have used and select those cards from your bibliography card collection.

*Bibliography form.*

1. Arrange in alphabetical order, according to author or editor (or title, if the work is anonymous).

2. Place last names first, followed by the title of the work in italics (underlined), and the publication data. Page numbers are not required.

3. Use periods between each main item.

4. Indent by five spaces the second and subsequent lines of the entry.

5. End the entry with a period.

6. If you have two books by the same author, do not repeat the author's name for the second entry. Instead, type an eight-space line ending with a period.

> Woolf, Virginia, *Mrs. Dalloway.* New York: Harcourt, Brace, 1925.
>     *The Years.* New York: Harcourt, Brace, 1937.

## Model Entries:
## Bibliography and First Footnote Reference

*BOOKS*
1. *A book with one author*

   Bibliography: Morris, Edmund. *The Rise of Theodore Roosevelt.* New York: Ballantine Books, 1979.

   First footnote: [1]Edmund Morris, *The Rise of Theodore Roosevelt* (New York: Ballantine Books, 1979), p. 273

   Second and later footnotes: [2]Morris, p. 274.

2. *A book with two authors*

   Bibliography: Barnet, Sylvan, and Marcia Stubbs. *Barnet and Stubb's Practical Guide to Writing.* Boston: Little, Brown and Company, 1977.

   First footnote: [2]Sylvan Barnet and Marcia Stubbs, *Barnet and Stubb's Practical Guide to Writing* (Boston: Little, Brown and Company, 1977), pp. 341-42.

   Second and later footnotes: [2]Barnet and Stubbs, p. 343.

3. *A book by three authors*

   Bibliography: Child, Julia, Louisette Bertholle, and Simone Beck. *Mastering the Art of French Cooking.* New York: Alfred A. Knopf, 1967.

   Footnote: [3]Julia Child, Louisette Bertholle, and Simone Beck, *Mastering the Art of French Cooking* (New York: Alfred A. Knopf, 1967), p. 300.

4. *A book by three or more authors* and *a book in a series*

   Bibliography: Osgood, Robert E., et al. America and the World, Volume II. *Retreat from Empire*. Baltimore: Johns Hopkins University Press, 1973.

   Footnote: [4]Robert E. Osgood, et al., America and the World, Volume II *Retreat from Empire* (Baltimore: Johns Hopkins University Press, 1973), p.96.

   Second and later footnote: [4]Osgood et al., p. 97.

NOTE: "Et al." stands for *et alii,* "and others." You may use the English equivalent if you like.

The word "The" is customarily omitted from publishers' names.

5. *A book by an editor*

   Bibliography: Hoffman, Ted, ed. *Famous American Plays of the 1970's.* New York: Dell Publishing Co., 1981.

   Footnote: [5]Ted Hoffman, ed., *Famous American Plays of the 1970's* (New York: Dell Publishing Co., 1981), p. 12.

   Second and later footnotes: [5]Hoffman, p. 13.

6. *A book by two editors*

   Bibliography: Liu, Wu-chi, and Irving Yucheng Lo, eds. *Sunflower Splendor: Three Thousand Years of Chinese Poetry.* New York: Doubleday, Anchor Press, 1975.

   Footnote: [6]Wu-chi Liu and Irving Yucheng, Lo, eds., *Sunflower Splendor: Three Thousand Years of Chinese Poetry* (New York: Doubleday, Anchor Press, 1975), p. 273.

   Second and Later Footnotes: [6]Liu and Yucheng, p. 274.

NOTE: This footnote makes reference to an earlier hardbound edition by Doubleday.

You do not need to give subtitles unless—as in this case—a subtitle clarifies the content of the work.

7. *An article from an edited anthology*

   Bibliography: O'Flaherty, J. Daniel. "Finding Jamaica's Way." *Developing Country Debt.* Edited by Lawrence G. Franko and Marilyn Seiber. New York: Pergamon Press, 1979.

   Footnote: [7]J. Daniel O'Flaherty, "Finding Jamaica's Way," in *Developing Country Debt*, eds. Lawrence G. Franko and Marilyn Seiber (New York: Pergamon Press, 1979), p. 135-36.

   Second and later footnotes: [7]O'Flaherty p. 137.

**8.** *A translation*

Bibliography: Aleixandre, Vicente. A *Longing for the Light: Selected Poems by Vicente Aleixandre*. Trans. Lewis Hyde. New York: Harper & Row, 1979.

Footnote: [8]Vicente Aleixandre, *A Longing for the Light: Selected Poems by Vicente Aleixandre*, trans. Lewis Hyde (New York: Harper & Row, 1979), p. 100

Second and later footnotes: [7]Aleixandre, p. 101.

**9.** *A book with an anonymous author*

Bibliography: *Beowulf: A Verse Translation into Modern English*. Trans. Edwin Morgan. Berkeley: University of California Press, 1962.

Footnote: [9]*Beowulf: A Verse Translation into Modern English*, trans. Edwin Morgan (Berkeley: University of California Press, 1962), p. 55.

Second and later footnotes: [9]*Beowulf*, p. 56.

## PERIODICALS AND NEWSPAPERS

**10.** *An article in a periodical with a volume number*

Bibliography: Snow, Richard F. "Melvil Dewey." *American Heritage*, 32, (Winter 1980).

Footnotes: [10]Richard F. Snow, "Melvil Dewey," *American Heritage*, 32, (Winter 1980), 72.

Second and later footnotes: [10]Snow, p. 72.

NOTE: When both volume (32) and page number (72) are given, as in this case, omit the words *Vol.* and *p.* or *pp.*

It is not necessary to give the issue number unless the periodical is only numbered by issue.

**11.** *A signed article in a weekly magazine*

Bibliography: Kael, Pauline. "Chance/Fate." *New Yorker*, 6 April 1981, pp. 154-166.

Footnote: [11]Pauline Kael, "Chance/Fate," *New Yorker*, 6 April 1981, p. 155

NOTE: Since no volume number is given, *p.* is used.

**12.** *A signed newspaper article*

Bibliography: Lardner, Ring Jr. "A Farewell to Hollywood." *The Washington Post*, 19 April 1981, p. B1, col. 1

Footnote: [12]Ring Lardner, Jr., "A Farewell to Hollywood," *The Washington Post*, 19 April 1981, p. B1, col. 1

NOTE: Since this newspaper is numbered by section, the section number is given. Newspaper column numbers are given for easy reference; columns are numbered right to left.

**13.** *An unsigned, untitled newspaper article*

Bibliography: *Wall Street Journal.* 22 May 1970, p. 1, col. 1

Footnote: [13]*Wall Street Journal,* 22 May 1970, p. 1, col. 1

Second and later footnotes: [13]*Wall Street Journal,* p.7

**14.** *An unpublished dissertation*

Bibliography: Hartmann, Heidi I. "Capitalism and Women's Work in the Home." Diss. Yale University, 1974.

Footnote: [14]Heidi I. Hartman, "Capitalism and Women's Work in the Home," Diss. Yale University, 1974, p. 40.

Second and later footnotes: [14]Hartman, p. 41.

**15.** *An article in an encyclopedia*

Bibliography: "England." *Encyclopedia Brittanica,* 1967.

Footnote: [15]"England, *Encyclopedia Brittanica,* 1967.

Second and later footnotes: [15]"England," p. 554.

NOTE: If the article is signed, begin the entry with the author's name, just as you would for a book or periodical.

**16.** *Bulletins or pamphlets*

Bibliography: *Usury Laws, Their Nature, Expediency and Influence.* Economic Tract No. IV. New York: The Society for Political Education, 1881.

Footnotes: [16]*Usury Laws, Their Nature, Expediency and Influence,* Economic Tract No. IV (New York: The Society for Political Education, 1881) pp. 33-34.

Second and later footnotes: [16]*Usury Laws,* p. 50

**17.** *Multiple works by the same author*

If you are using two works by the same author, you must give the title in each footnote reference:

[3]Kael, "Chance/Fate," p. 156

[4]Kael, *Deeper into Movies,* p. 206.

**18.** *More than one citation if a work is on the same page*

If you have the second citation of a work on the same page of your text, you may use *ibid. Ibid.* stands for the Latin *ibidem,* "in the same place."

[3]Kael, "Chance/Fate," p. 156.

[4]Ibid.                    { The same work
                            and the same page

³Kael, "Chance/Fate," p. 156.

⁴Ibid, p. 157.

> The same work citing a different page

You cannot use *ibid.* to refer to a work cited on a previous page of your text. The author's name (and title of work, if necessary) must already have been referred to on the same page of your text.

## General Appearance

It's important to turn in a neatly typed, clean copy of your paper. Probably yours is not the only term paper your teacher is reading, so don't put yourself at a disadvantage by submitting a paper that is difficult to read. Be sure you leave ample margins and use a fresh typewriter ribbon.

After you have typed your paper, proofread it for typographical errors, omissions, or mistakes in form. Ask a friend to give it a second proofreading. Insert corrections neatly with a pen.

> neatly
> Insert corrections with a pen.
> ∧

### Typing

1. Use white, good quality bond paper, 8½ × 11 inches. Do not use erasable paper; it smudges and does not take a clear ink impression.

2. Use a black ribbon new enough to produce readable copy. Do not use colored ribbons.

3. Clean the typeface characters and make sure the typewriter is in good working order.

4. Double-space throughout, except for footnotes, bibliographic entries, and long quotations.

### Basic Form

1. Use margins of at least an inch on all four sides of the paper. Margins of 1¼ or 1½ inch would be preferable; the paper shouldn't look crammed. Put a light pencil mark at the bottom of the page to indicate the margin. Erase the mark later.

2. All pages in the paper are assigned numbers. However you do not mark the number on the title page and the first page of the body of the material. Preliminary materials — for example, the outline or table of contents — are numbered with small roman numerals beginning with (ii). The body of the paper is numbered with Arabic numerals, beginning with (2) on the second page. Thus, you might have:

| | | | |
|---|---|---|---|
| title page — | not marked | first page — | not marked |
| outline — | ii, iii, iv | second page — | 2 |

3. Numbers should be typed at the top of the page, either in the center or in the upper right-hand corner.

4. Provide a title page with your paper's title in capital letters and below that your name. In the lower third of the page, give the name of the course and the date the paper is due or submitted.

5. On the first page of the body of the paper, place the title of your paper, in capitals, two or three inches from the top. Begin the text one or two double spacings below that.

6. Fasten your paper in the upper left-hand corner with a paper clip or staple; stapling is more secure.

7. Do not use a paper or plastic binder; do not use a blank cover sheet. These covers are awkward for the teacher's use, preventing your teacher from seeing at a glance which papers he or she has in hand. It's a cordial gesture to provide a final, blank sheet of paper: your teacher can use the space to make comments.

## Punctuation

For fuller treatment of punctuation, please see pages 83-87.

1. Leave two spaces after a period, a question mark, or other end punctuation.

2. Leave one space after a comma, a semi-colon, and a colon.

3. Leave no spaces after the period in such abbreviations as: e.g., a.m., B.C., D.C., U.S.

4. Write a dash by typing two hyphens with no space before or after. A dash is used to provide emphasis.

   He found his brother—broke and miserable—living in a shack at the edge of town.

5. Indicate italics by underlining words; use the underlining key on the typewriter. Do not underline between words: <u>New Yorker</u>.

## Numbers

1. Spell out all numbers through one hundred:

   thirty-eight          fifty-five

2. Spell out all round numbers that can be expressed in one or two words:

   five thousand          thirty-five hundred

3. If several round numbers appear in a series, they may be expressed in figures:

   During the frost, 2,000 trees died, 3,500 were damaged and 4,000 survived.

4. Write as figures exact numbers over one hundred:

   365 days in a year

5. If both round and exact numbers appear in a closely related series, express all numbers as figures:

   Of those who went to the polls, 115 voted yes, 50 voted not, and 23 abstained on this issue.

6. A sentence should not begin with a figure. Either spell out the first number or rewrite the sentence.

   Three hundred and sixty-five days are in a year.

   There are 365 days in a year.

7. Express very large numbers as figures, in terms of millions or billions.

   4 million

   5.7 billion

*Abbreviations*

1. Abbreviate common titles such as Mr., Mrs., and Dr.

2. Spell out civil, military, religious, and professional titles preceding the surname:

   Senator Sarbanes    Professor Ford

But abbreviate before a full name:

   Sen. Paul Sarbanes    Prof. Pat Ford

3. Spell out directions such as north, south, east, west, northeast, etc. Capitalize when they are part of a name:

   south side of the street    on East Circle Drive

4. Spell out words like avenue, street, drive, and building. Capitalize when they are part of a name:

   the tree-lined avenue    the Empire State Building

5. Spell out names of months and days in the text. When they appear in the footnotes or bibliography, you may abbreviate:

   Jan., Feb., Mar., Apr., May, June, July,

   Aug., Sept., Oct., Nov., Dec.

   Mon., Tues., Wed., Thurs., Fri., Sat.

*Titles*

1. As a general rule, underline (put in italics) the titles of whole published works, and put in double quotation marks the titles of parts of works.

2. Underline the titles of books, periodicals, pamphlets, and bulletins.

3. Put in quotation marks titles of short stories, essays, articles, and chapters in books:

> "Old Red" is a short story by Caroline Gordon
>
> Emerson's essay, "Self-Reliance"
>
> Chapter Five is called "The Political Hack"
>
> "The Archeology of Foucault" in *New York Review of Books*

4. Do not underline or set in quotations the titles of sacred texts—Bible, Talmud, etc.

> The Revised Standard Version of the Bible

5. Set the titles of short poems in quotation marks:

> Keats's "Ode to Autumn"

Underline the titles of long poems:

> Paradise Lost
>
> The Canterbury Tales

6. Underline titles of paintings, drawings and sculpture: Rembrandt's painting Aristotle Contemplating the Bust of Homer

7. Underline titles of plays and motions pictures:

> Chekhov's The Cherry Orchard
>
> Birth of a Nation

8. Set in quotation marks the titles of radio and television programs:

> NPR's "All Things Considered"
>
> "The Mary Tyler Moore Show"

9. Underline titles of long musical compositions, such as symphonies, ballets, and operas:

Mozart's Jupiter Symphony

(Or: Symphony no. 41)

Verdi's Otello

Set in quotation marks titles of shorter musical pieces:

> Schubert's song "Ave Maria"

## Parts of Speech

There are eight parts of speech: *verb, noun, pronoun, adverb, adjective, conjunction, preposition,* and *interjection.* A part of speech is determined by the way it functions in a sentence. One word can serve as different parts of speech.

They watched ducks from behind a *blind*.        *noun*

The sun will *blind* you with its light.        *verb*

They found themselves in a *blind* alley.        *adjective*

## VERBS

A *verb* expresses <u>doing</u> or <u>being</u>:

think, sit, sleep, read, discuss, give, escape, remember, mix, be

A verb can also make a <u>statement</u>, give a <u>command</u>, or ask a <u>question</u>:

It was him                Leave at once.                Are you well?

## NOUNS

A *noun* is a naming word. It names <u>people, places, things</u>. It also names <u>ideas, emotions</u>, and <u>qualities</u>.

gypsy, grocer, farmer, guest, father, highway, river, museum, den, sandwich, tiger, boat, philosophy, faith, happiness, cruelty

A *proper noun* names a <u>particular thing</u>, and is <u>capitalized</u>.

My favorite uncle is Uncle Lou.

The Metropolitan Museum is the largest museum in town.

## PRONOUNS

A *pronoun* <u>takes the place of a noun</u>.

Helen is a good cook. *She* cooks ravioli.

George said that *he* refused to dance.

The Jacksons were tired; *they* had driven all night.

Pronoun forms:

I, me, my, mine, myself, we, us, our, ours, ourselves, you, your, yours, yourself, yourselves, he, him, his, himself, she, her, hers, herself, they, them, their, theirs, themselves, it, itself

It must be made unmistakably clear to which noun the pronoun refers.

CLEAR:     People were eager to see the juggler. *They* were not disappointed.

People were eager to see the juggler. *He* was a great success.

UNCLEAR:     Mr. Tucci told Mr. Singer his novels were clever.

It's unclear whether the novels of Mr. Tucci or Mr. Singer are being referred to.

REVISED: Mr. Tucci explained *he* admired Mr. Singer's novels.

UNCLEAR: The waiter took the customer's order when he was crying.

REVISED: The waiter was crying when *he* took the customer's order.

UNCLEAR: After Nick's fish was weighed, he took a picture of it.

A pronoun must refer to a noun (not, as in this case, to the modifier *Nick's.*)

REVISED: After his fish was weighed, *Nick* took a picture of it.

UNCLEAR: Mr. and Mrs. Banks took his car to the garage.

REVISED: Mr. and Mrs. Banks took *their* car to the garage.

A pronoun must agree in number and gender with the noun it replaces.

WRONG: An astronaut is often asked questions about their experience in space.

REVISED: An astronaut is often asked about *his* experience in space.

Use a *singular pronoun* to refer to such words as: each, one, no one, either, neither, another, anyone, anybody, someone, somebody, everybody, everyone, nobody, person, kind, sort.

Someone carved his name on the elm tree.

Somebody left her high heels at the party.

Everyone will make his own choice.

Each girl in the group voted to bring her favorite book.

Use <u>it</u> to refer to places and things, and to collective nouns such as: assembly, group, army, school, audience.

---

**EXERCISE**

Choose the correct pronoun.

1. A cook and a baker have opened a shop to sell_____goods.

2. Anyone can learn to cut_____own hair.

3. Politicians sometimes express amazement when _____are asked for an opinion.

4. The club voted on_____constitution.

5. One can find the bluebird of happiness in _____own backyard.

6. Sally and Fran brought the pig _____had raised.

7. No one dies from having_____heart broken.

8. During the tornado, the house lost _____roof.

---

## ADVERBS

An *adverb* modifies — tells more about — <u>verbs</u>, <u>other adverbs</u>, and <u>adjectives</u>. Many adverbs end in *-ly*.

Adverbs modifying verbs:

> The corn is growing *rapidly*.

> Mammals appeared *late* in the Mesozoic era.

> He called *softly* through the window.

> They entered the room *noisily*.

Adverbs modifying other adverbs:

> He called *very* softly through the window.

> The corn is growing *so* rapidly.

> They gave the money *somewhat* reluctantly.

Adverbs modifying adjectives:

> The cellist has a *terribly* old instrument.

> You can have this *slightly* worn out book.

> She received a *neatly* folded letter.

> The *angrily* shouting crowd turned back.

## ADJECTIVES

An *adjective* modifies — tells more about — a noun or pronoun.

> Take a cup of *hot* chocolate.

> The *little, red* car pulled up.

> The *comic* novel is still thriving.

> Here are *ten* cents.

*Few people are willing to study that hard.*

*Many* students will drop out.

The *bespectacled, shy* sailor smiled at us.

He was *handsome.*

If an adjective comes from a proper noun, it must be capitalized:

English muffin

Jeffersonian democracy

French wine

Marxist philosophy

---

## EXERCISE

Identify the adjectives and adverbs as follows:

    *adv.*         *adj.*

He sailed rapidly in his yellow boat.

1. They danced gracefully around the large ballroom.

2. After hours in the cold ocean, they felt very tired.

3. Little knots of tired watchers gathered quietly on the beach.

4. Sifting very gently through the sand, the eager archeologist found the artifact.

5. He spoke so softly to old Mrs. Fenn, she could barely hear him.

6. The town was dark, the house lights faintly glimmering.

7. He insisted on wearing deliberately somber clothes.

8. She handed him fifty cents and hastily departed.

---

## CONJUNCTIONS

A *conjunction* connects words and groups of words that are of equal rank.

and = means an addition

but = introduces a contrast

or = introduces an alternative

Say hello to Agnes *and* Bob.

The stones *and* trees have been cleared away.

We went to Chinatown *and* then we went on a boat ride around the bay.

She likes biography, *but* he prefers thrillers.

Not apples *but* oranges are more nutritious.

Invest now *or* you may regret it later.

Should I stay inside *or* go sailing?


## PREPOSITIONS

A *preposition* is always the first word in a <u>prepositional phrase</u>. A preposition is followed by a noun or pronoun, which is called the <u>object</u>.

<u>at</u> the corner  <u>with</u> a moment to spare  <u>for</u> the love <u>of</u> Mike
  <u>obj.</u>      <u>obj.</u>      <u>obj.</u>  <u>obj.</u>

Here are some common prepositions:

at, by, before, behind, between, of, for, from, during, before, after in front of, on, over, through, above, below, beyond, beside, across, under

A prepositional phrase can modify a noun or a verb.

Turn on the lamp *beside the door.*

The woman *in the red dress* burst out laughing.

There is a china shop *over the grocery.*

It rained *during the tennis match.*

Mr. Riggs lives *in the cabin on the lake.*

They drove *at top speed.*

Notice that a prepositional phrase often contains adjectives that modify the noun, or object. For example, in the sentence above, the prepositional phrase *during the tennis match* modifies rained (explains when it rained). The word *tennis* modifies match (tells what kind of match).

When a pronoun is the object of the preposition, it must appear in the right form (the objective case).

| WRONG: | in front of I | RIGHT: | between you and me |
|--------|---------------|--------|--------------------|
| RIGHT: | in front of me | WRONG: | among we intellectuals |
| WRONG: | between you and I | RIGHT: | among us intellectuals |

**EXERCISE**

Choose the proper form for the pronouns in the prepositional phrases.

1. Did you call to (I, me)?

2. A car slid to a halt in front of (him, he).

3. Nobody cares about (us, we) farmers.

4. There was a basket of fruit waiting for (me, I).

5. A dove and two fawns appeared before (she, her).

6. There was an argument between (he, him) and (I, me).

NOTE: *among* and *between:*

> You sit *between* two people.          You sit *among* three or more.

## INTERJECTIONS

An *interjection* is a short emphatic expression of emotion. It is commonly used in speech and informal writing. It is rarely appropriate in a term paper. When appearing alone, an interjection is usually followed by an exclamation mark.

> Help!          Hello!          Alas!          Hurrah!

An interjection can also appear as part of the sentence, in which case it is punctuated with commas.

> Oh, I long for the good old days.

> It was, alas, neither the right time nor the right place.

## *Avoid Sentence Fragments*

A *sentence* may be long or short, simple or complex, but it must have a *subject* and a *verb* to be complete.

> Cats sleep.

> The works of great poets are an inspiration.

The subject of a sentence may be implied.

Sometimes when a verb gives a command, the subject of the sentence—*you*—is implied, or understood to be present. However, you cannot imply both the subject and the verb.

INCORRECT:     Care to dance?          "You" and "do' both implied

CORRECT:        Dance with me.          "You" implied

| INCORRECT: | Have some tea? | *"You"* and *"will"* implied |
| CORRECT: | Go to the corner and turn left. | *"You"* implied |
| CORRECT: | Ask for help whenever possible. | *"You"* implied |
| CORRECT: | Get some sleep for your health. | *"You"* implied |

A *sentence* may have <u>two or more subjects</u> and <u>two or more verbs</u>.

<u>We</u> <u>ate</u> everything on the table and <u>slept</u> until dawn.

<u>Thompson</u> <u>read</u> several books and <u>wrote</u> a report on one.

<u>We</u> <u>swam</u>, <u>sailed</u>, and <u>hiked</u>.

The <u>ranchers</u> and the <u>sheepherders</u> <u>argued</u>.

The <u>doctors</u>, <u>interns</u>, and <u>nurses</u> <u>were</u> tired.

The <u>students</u> and the <u>teachers</u> <u>marched</u> on stage and <u>sang</u> the college song.

A sentence must make sense by itself. It must express a complete thought. A *sentence fragment* does not make sense by itself. Sentence fragments are often used in informal conversation:

Back so soon?                Flew in Thursday!                Great!

In formal writing such as the term paper, the sentence fragment should not be used.

FRAGMENT: Books sitting in their dusty rows.

CORRECTED: Books were sitting in their dusty rows.

Books should be sitting in their dusty rows.

FRAGMENT: Love at first sight.

CORRECTED: It was love at first sight.

FRAGMENT: To see Paris in the spring.

CORRECTED: He wanted to see Paris in the spring.

FRAGMENT: When he plays the violin.

CORRECTED: They applaud when he plays the violin.

FRAGMENT: Going to New York to seek his fortune.

CORRECT: Jim was going to New York to seek his fortune.

NOTICE that verbs ending in *-ing* cannot function as the verb without helping verbs.

FRAGMENTED:   I going.

CORRECTED:     I am going.

FRAGMENTED:   Horses galloping through the field.

CORRECTED:     Horses were galloping through the field.

Remember, a verb form ending in -*ing* — called the gerund — can function as a noun.

Swimming is fun.

Lending books can be a mistake.

---

## EXERCISE

In the list below, identify the complete sentences with a check and the sentence fragments with an *F*. In the complete sentences, underline the subject and double underline the verb.

EXAMPLE:     ✔ I have been cutting corners.

F    Because she was late.

1. Nobody knows.

2. Returning from a trip with her aunt.

3. Mr. Dale, after some thought, planted a rose garden.

4. In the event of snow.

5. In case of snow, call me.

6. What is your name?

7. Bums lingering in doorways.

8. On the highways, on the roads, and on the country lanes.

9. In a rush, the teacher arriving just in time.

10. Something to see in every room.

---

Sometimes a group of words may contain a subject and a verb and still not make sense by itself. If a group of words is introduced by certain marker words, it is a *subordinate clause*. These are the marker words that signal that a group of words is a subordinate clause, and not a complete sentence. These are called *subordinating conjunctions*. Following are some examples:

that, what, which, who, whoever, whom, whomever, whose (these are called relative pronouns) after, although, as, as if, as though, because, before, if, in order that, since, so that, that, though, unless, until, when, whatever, whenever, where, wherever, while

A subordinate clause does not make sense by itself. It is dependent on the *main clause*.

| MAIN CLAUSE | | SUBORDINATE CLAUSE |
|---|---|---|
| He jogged | + | because he enjoyed it. |
| Everything was fine | + | until the storm broke. |
| She admits | + | that she was too hasty. |
| The party got better | + | after the band arrived. |

A subordinate clause can come at the beginning or in the middle of a sentence.

| SUBORDINATE CLAUSE | | MAIN CLAUSE |
|---|---|---|
| Unless he practices more | + | he will not be a good player. |
| Before we take the drive | + | we should wash the car. |

| SUBJECT | SUBORDINATE CLAUSE | VERB |
|---|---|---|
| The book, | which was rare, | was expensive. |

If a group of words introduced by a marker word stands by itself, it is a sentence fragment, *not* a sentence. For example:

> When he sings.

When he sings—what? The dogs bark? He weeps? People throw money? We don't know, because the sentence fragment is like an unanswered question. When you look for sentence completeness, ask yourself if the sentence leaves any unanswered questions.

---

## EXERCISE

In the list below, identify the complete sentences with a check and the sentence fragments with an *F*. In the complete sentences, underline the subject and double underline the verb. Put brackets [    ] around the subordinate clauses.

EXAMPLE:

✔    [Because he was afraid,] he hid.

F    Until the cows come home.

1. Although the day was warm, Jenkins wore a heavy sweater.

2. Since you like chocolate so much.

3. She goes to the movies whenever she can.

4. He is a farmer who also paints pictures.

5. Where the road turns left and the sign has fallen down.

6. That Smith boy, coming down the hill.

**7.** In order to form a perfect union.

**8.** The soldiers, after marching all night, were forced to march all day.

**9.** It is a place which relaxes you.

---

Sometimes a fragment is part of an adjacent sentence, and can be attached to that sentence to form a complete sentence.

| | |
|---|---|
| FRAGMENT: | You mustn't lose your balance. Even for a moment. |
| CORRECTED: | You mustn't lose your balance, even for a moment. |
| FRAGMENT: | He was a comic sight. Like Santa Claus on the Fourth of July. |
| CORRECTED: | He was a comic sight, like Santa Claus on the Fourth of July. |

---

## EXERCISE

Eliminate each sentence fragment below by repunctuating it and attaching it to the preceding or following sentence.

**1.** I saw nobody I knew. So I looked around the rehearsal room.

**2.** The chorus was assembled on stage. Singing its heart out.

**3.** The producer called a break. To give them a chance to rest.

**4.** Just a few more minutes! Then my turn would come.

**5.** Like a scared kid. I opened my mouth and nothing came out.

**6.** At last. The director cried, "Bravo!"

---

## Avoid Run-On Sentences

A common *sentence error* is the run-on sentence. In a run-on sentence, two sentences are linked with only a comma (comma splice) or with no punctuation (fused sentence). Conjunctions such as *and* or *but* are absent between the two sentences.

*RUN-ON:* Cats are sleeping on the porch, dogs are barking in the yard.

There are three common ways to correct the run-on sentence.

**1.** Use a period and make two sentences.

Cats are sleeping on the porch. Dogs are barking in the yard.

**2.** Use a semicolon. A semicolon is used between two complete sentences with closely related ideas.

Cats are sleeping on the porch; dogs are barking in the yard.

3. Use a comma and the conjunctions *and* or *but*.

> Cats are sleeping on the porch, and the dogs are barking in the yard.

You may also subordinate one part of the sentence by introducing it with a subordinating conjunction like *while, after, when, whenever, because,* etc. A subordinating conjunction signals that the words that follow it are *not* a complete sentence.

> Cats are sleeping on the porch, while dogs are barking in the yard.

---

## EXERCISE

Correct the following run-on sentences by using one of the methods suggested above.

1. He was a hard-working man, his family depended on him.
2. The youngest boy left home after high school he joined the navy.
3. The schoolhouse could have burned down, the fire truck arrived just in time.
4. The elms on Travers Street died, the willows in the park flourished.
5. On Saturday afternoons, we mowed the lawns and pruned the hedge, at night we just loafed.

---

## Verbs and Verb Functions

A verb may consist of a verb phrase; *main verb + helping verb.*

Helping verbs are such words as: <u>be, is, am, was, were, do, does, did, should, shall, can, could, may, might, must, have, has, had.</u>

> I *have had* a doughnut.
>
> He *is going* to Detroit.
>
> The waiter *should have served* them earlier.
>
> Aunt Rae *must have been* upset.
>
> They *were singing* an old sea chanty.

Words formed from verbs, enging in *-ing,* and functioning as nouns are called *gerunds.*

> *Swimming* is good for you.
>
> It's hard to do a lot of *sweeping.*
>
> I could never get him to do any *snorkeling.*

Words formed from verbs, ending in -*ing* or -*ed* and functioning as adjectives are called *participles*.

> Sitting on the porch, she began to read.

*Sitting* modifies *she; on the porch,* a prepositional phrase, modifies *sitting*.

---

Words formed from verbs and used chiefly as a nouns, sometimes as an adjective, are called *infinitives*. Infinitives began with *to* and are completed by the present tense of the verb.

> to watch
> to do
> to research
>
> I tried to swim.

The infinitive phrase *to swim* is the object of the verb *tried*.

Some words, called *particles,* act with verbs to complete the verb's meaning. Particles are such words as *across, after, in, up, off, on, down, over, out*. Particles function as a unit with the verb.

> He is *taking off*.
>
> She *is giving up*.

Learn to distinguish words associated with verbs from the verbs themselves.

> I do not *wish* to go.

*Not* modifies the verb; it is an adverb, not a verb. *To go* is an infinitive phrase.

---

**EXERCISE**

Identify the verbs in the following passage by underlining them twice.

> We started out climbing the mountain at six in the morning. Tom and Nancy carried the packs, but we switched after Tom got tired. It was a beautiful clear morning. The wind ruffled our clothes. The path up the mountain rose steeply at one point, and we were gasping for breath. There was nothing to do but go on. Dozens of birds were calling and whistling. We surprised a barred owl who flapped soundlessly away. Nancy collected a salamander, which did not amuse me. Tom wouldn't look at it. At noon, we collapsed under an oak tree and munched our sandwiches. Nancy played her harmonica and Tom quoted Wordsworth to us. I said, "I climb, therefore I am."

---

Some verbs are called *linking verbs*. They link the subject of the sentence with a noun, noun substitute, or adjective which gives us more information about the subject.

> She *is* beautiful.

He *is* a cowboy.

The water *tasted* wonderful.

Linking verbs are the verbs of the five senses and verbs of being:

look, feel, smell, sound, taste

be, am, are, is, was, were, seem,

become, appear, grow, stay, remain

---

**EXERCISE**

Identify the *linking verbs* in the following sentences.

1. The lake, usually choppy, remained calm.

2. The sun grew warm on our backs.

3. The homemade fudge tasted delicious.

4. At first, he hated the opera, but later he became a fan.

5. The building was old and deserted.

6. After he mortgaged his home, he felt sad.

---

Some verbs, called *transitive verbs,* take an object to complete their meaning. The *object* receives the action of the verb.

He *kicked* the mailbox.
object

He *read* the book.
object

She *capsized* the boat.
object

She *got up* early and *baked* bread.
object

The object which receives the direct action of the verb is a *direct object*. An *indirect object* indirectly receives the action of the verb.

She <u>baked</u> him a loaf of bread
↑
indirect object

He <u>sent</u> her a bill.
↑
indirect object

An indirect object states *to whom, to what, for whom,* or *for what* something is done. Therefore, you can usually substitute a prepositional phrase for an indirect object.

She baked a loaf of bread for him.

He sent a bill to her.

To identify the direct object in a sentence, ask: Who or what is being acted upon? To identify the indirect object, ask: Who or what will be the indirect recipient of that action?

The politician mailed the voters a brochure.

What is being mailed? Not the voters—the brochure. To whom is it being mailed? The voters.

---

**EXERCISE**

In the sentences below, label the following: the subject, verb, direct object, indirect object (if any).

EXAMPLE:

i.o. = indirect object

She gave him a kiss.
i.o.

1. Harry's friends brought him a houseplant.

2. Mrs. Noble taught him his ABC's.

3. The Hendersons and the Smiths played golf.

4. In the moonlight, Bill was playing Sue old songs on his guitar.

5. They ignited a bonfire after the game.

6. After returning from Spain, they gave Paris a second chance.

---

The subject of a sentence must *agree* with its verb *in number*. A singular subject requires a singular verb. A plural subject requires a plural verb.

One person *is* fine.

Two people *are* fine.

---

**EXERCISE**

Choose the correct verb form by underlining it.

1. The firemen (are rescuing, is rescuing) the cat in the tree.

2. A single rose (cose, costs) one dollar.

3. A stitch in time (saves, save) nine.

4. Athletes in training (exercise, exercises) regularly.

5. Opinions about the movie (vary, varies) greatly.

6. The questions on the examination (were, was) easy.

---

Two or more subjects joined by <u>and</u> are treated as a plural and take a plural verb.

> Smith and Green were the first to arrive.
>
> (Compare to: Smith was the first to arrive.)
>
> Flour, salt, and yeast are the essential ingredients.

In sentences where the subject is connected by *or* or *either/or* or *neither/nor* constructions are used, the verb must agree with subject *nearer* to it.

> Love or good grades *are* the answer.
>
> Good grades or love *is* the answer.
>
> Neither Fred nor his parents *are* present.
>
> Neither his parents or Fred *is* present.
>
> Either Mary or her sisters *are* going to sing.
>
> Either her sisters or Mary *is* going to sing.

---

## EXERCISE

Choose the correct verb form by underlining it.

1. Neither the florists nor the jeweler (are, is) paying their bills.

2. Geometry and spelling (is, are) her weaknesses.

3. Either a book or flowers (is, are) an appropriate gift.

4. Neither junk food nor sweets (is, are) good for you.

5. The tree and the shrubs (is, are) to be cut down.

6. Paper and a pencil (are, is) necessary.

---

Be careful when a group of words comes between the subject and the verb. You can find the true subject by ignoring the intervening words.

> This book [of sonnets] is Mary's.
>
> The farmers [who delivered the milk to the store] are returning late.
>
> The cause [of the fires] is unknown.

---

## EXERCISE

Choose the correct verb by ignoring intervening words. Underline your choice.

1. This bookcase full of books (appear, appears) to be oak.

2. A convention of mayors (is, are) meeting at the hotel.

3. The runner who came in first in two races (is, are) getting a prize.

4. The streets of Washington, D.C. (is, are) clean.

5. The members of the garment workers union (is, are) on strike.

6. The children who acted in the play (were, was) given prizes.

---

Collective nouns are treated as a single unit and take a singular verb. Nouns singular in meaning, though plural in form, take a singular verb.

The jury is still undecided.

The two-car family is a thing of the past.

A flock of geese was flying north.

A congregation was on its knees.

The crowd of well-wishers was growing impatient.

"Number" is a singular noun.

Mathematics was the composer's hobby.

The news is good.

Economics is not well understood.

Sentences beginning there is, there are, here is, and here are allow the subject to come after the verb. Do not confuse the adverbs there and here with the subject.

There are a thousand extras in the film.

There is one good reason for not smoking.

Here are the twins.

Here is the train.

There were numerous complaints.

There was a tramp at the door.

Here were the homes of the Indians.

Here was the spot where I was born.

When used as a subject, the following words require a *singular verb:* each, either, neither, one, no one, nobody, nothing, anyone, anybody, anything, everyone, everybody, everything, someone, somebody.

The following words may take either a singular or a plural verb, depending on the context: none, some, all, any, more, most.

Nobody has an exclusive claim on the truth.

Everyone has the same chance at happiness.

One plays as well as the other.

Each was asked to do his part.

Some of the cookies were chocolate chip.

Some of the food was raw.

Most of the students are rebellious.

Most of the book is well-written.

None of it is missing.

None of the flowers have bloomed.

---

## EXERCISE

Choose the correct verb form. Underline your choice.

1. Here (is, are) the answer to Danby's question

2. There (is, are) several delicious pastries available.

3. Each of us (have, has) special prejudices.

4. Neither of them (has, have) forgotten the incident.

5. Some of the buildings (were, was) in ruins.

6. Everybody who learns to ski (falls, fall) at some time.

7. Linguistics (is, are) the study of language.

8. One often (think, thinks) of returning home.

9. There (is, are) guests staying at Mrs. Monroe's house.

10. The army (are receiving, is receiving) its orders.

---

*Regular verbs* form the past tense by adding *-ed* or *d* to the present.

I walk. I walked.

I like. I liked.

But *irregular verbs* form the past tense by changing their spelling or using a different word.

| I write. | I wrote. |
| I go. | I went. |
| I find. | I found. |

TWENTY IRREGULAR VERBS.

| PRESENT | | PAST | |
|---|---|---|---|
| awake | freeze | awoke | froze |
| become | hang (suspend) | became | hung |
| bid (offer) | hang (execute) | bid | hanged |
| bid (command) | lay (put down) | bade, bid | laid |
| blow | lie (recline) | blew | lay |
| burst | raise (lift) | burst | raised |
| dive | rise (get up) | dived, dove | rose |
| drag | set (place) | dragged | set |
| draw | sit | drew | sat |
| drink | take | drank | took |

---

## EXERCISE

Choose the correct past tense form.

1. Yesterday, a celebrated criminal was (hang) _____

2. Last year, the museum (hang) _____ all its nineteenth century paintings in one room.

3. Because he was so tired, he (lie) _____ down.

4. He ran to the edge of the pool and (dive) _____ into the water.

5. When Myrna got up to leave, all of her friends also (rise) _____

6. He (drag) _____ her off, kicking and screaming.

---

## *Avoid Dangling Modifiers*

A word or group of words intended to modify another word in a sentence is called a *modifier*. The modifier must always clearly refer to a word in the sentence; if it does not, it is called a *dangling modifier*.

In order to avoid dangling modifiers, remember this guideline: A modifier must always refer to a word in the sentence you can point to.

DANGLING     Arrving on time, the party had already started.

Did the party arrive on time? The modifier "arriving on time" does not refer to a word in the sentence.

REVISED     Arriving on time, we found the party had already started.

DANGLING     While sitting on deck chairs, the steward served hot drinks.

Was the steward sitting in deck chairs? No.

REVISED    While sitting on deck chairs, we were served hot drinks by the steward.

OR

While we sat on deck chairs, the steward served hot drinks.

DANGLING    Running on the sand, my hat fell off.

Did the hat run on the sand? No.

REVISED    Running on the sand, I lost my hat.

---

## EXERCISE

Revise the following sentences, eliminating the dangling modifiers.

1. After taking off at a gallop, we cheered for our favorite horses.

2. By eating all the right foods, your hair can be shiny and your skin clear.

3. Playing only Beethoven, the concert was a huge success.

4. While becoming increasingly worried, the hours passed.

5. Having been caught for speeding, the traffic cop gave the young man a ticket.

6. After meditation, your body will be more relaxed.

---

## *Punctuation*

### COMMAS

A *comma* separates words and groups of words to clarify meaning. The comma is the least emphatic of all punctuation marks, but it is often essential to the readability of sentences.

Use a comma to separate a long clause or phrase at the beginning of a sentence.

Whenever he called her on the telephone, she hung up on him.

After months and years had passed, the city was rebuilt.

If the waitresses had formed a union, they could have gotten better wages.

Use a comma to separate words in a series. In a series of three or more, commas are required between each element and after the last one.

She liked baubles, bangles, and beads.

A national favorite is a hamburger, French fries, and cola.

Use a comma before and/or/but joining two main clauses.

We huddled around the camp fire, and Betty insisted on playing her ukelele.

We had never before flown in a transatlantic jet, or visited a foreign country.

Miss Cantor had never visited Paris before, but she had been speaking French all her life.

Use a comma between adjectives

It was a hot, sunny afternoon.

The building was tall, grey, massive.

Use a comma to set off parenthetical elements which are not essential to the meaning of the sentence. Do not use a comma to set off groups of words which are essential to the meaning of the sentence. A parenthetical element can be ommited and the sentence will still convey its meaning.

| PARENTHETICAL | Students, for example, usually procrastinate. |
| ESSENTIAL | Students usually procrastinate. |
| PARENTHETICAL | The captain, who was wearing a blue blazer, showed us his maps. |
| ESSENTIAL | The player who was wearing number nine made the final goal. |
| PARENTHETICAL | My daughter, who is majoring in English, is an only child. |
| ESSENTIAL | My daughter who is at college is coming home this weekend. |
| PARENTHETICAL | Books, which are sometimes read for instruction, are really a source of pleasure. |
| ESSENTIAL | Books which are read for instruction can be useful. |

The comma may be omitted between two short main clauses.

The moon was full and the night was cold.

The trucks rumbled and the cars roared.

A comma should not be used between two verbs sharing a subject.

| FAULTY | The bear saw the woman, and lumbered off. |
| REVISED | The bear saw the woman and lumbered off. |

| FAULTY | Jane Austen sat in her family's parlor, and wrote her novels. |
|---|---|
| REVISED | Jane Austen sat in her family's parlor and wrote her novels. |

---

## EXERCISE

Punctuate these sentences with commas where necessary. Omit unnecessary commas by drawing a circle around them.

1. It was alas my last dollar.

2. After leaving him at the train station, I strolled home alone.

3. Cats prowled and dogs slept.

4. The teacher who was least liked was voted most unpopular.

5. Mr. Thomas, who recently returned from Tahiti, is giving a slide show for the P.T.A.

6. This is my uncle, who is a baker, and this is my uncle, who is a broker.

7. He bought a set of postcards, an old chair and a desk.

8. Before the anthem was sung at exactly six o'clock the organ played a musical medley.

9. He sported a trimmed pointed goatee.

10. Horses which can be raced can also be eaten.

---

## SEMICOLONS

A semicolon is more emphatic than a comma. It is used to join two clauses of equal rank. Two clauses, each with a subject and a verb, must be joined by a semicolon if they are not joined by a conjunction.

| CONJUNCTION | The moon had just begun to rise, and we were on our way at last. |
|---|---|
| SEMICOLON | The moon had just begun to rise; we were on our way at last. |

Do *not* use a semicolon to join unlike clauses.

| FAULTY | I like my history course; I had the same art teacher last year. |
|---|---|

---

## EXERCISE

Join the following sentences with a semicolon.

1. The idea of infinity is a wonder to us. We can hardly comprehend it.

2. Cowboys invented the rodeo. The range was their first arena.

3. Taxi drivers are born philosophers. Opinions are their daily bread.

4. The ferry boat churned out of the harbor. Behind us, lay our past.

5. Dancers eat yogurt and get up at dawn. Actors eat junk food and rise at noon.

6. He didn't want to keep his job. He wanted to run off like an irresponsible kid.

---

A semicolon must set off two main clauses. In other words, there must be a subject and a verb on both sides of the semicolon.

> FAULTY: She listened to his advice; and took it to heart.

> REVISED: She listened to his advice; she took it to heart.

> FAULTY: The paintings were very rare; and cost him too much.

> REVISED: The paintings were very rare; they cost him too much.

> or

> The paintings were very rare and cost him too much.

## COLONS

A colon is a break in the continuity of the sentence. It introduces a clause or a phrase that emphasizes, clarifies, or explains what went before it. A colon is highly formal and should not be used needlessly.

> Love can have many facets: affection, jealousy, friendship, romance.

> He could identify three problems with the new machine: mechanical, electronic, chemical.

## PARENTHESES

*Parentheses* are used to set off explanatory, or qualifying remarks. Marks punctuating the sentence fall *outside* the parentheses.

> Mr. Teale had a clear notion of the first step (although no notion at all of the second).

> Most states (with the exception of New York) do not have rent stabilization laws.

## QUOTATION MARKS

*Quotation marks* set off direct quotations and some titles.

> The story I liked best in Eudora Welty's *The Golden Apples* was "Moon Lake."

Should we go see *Rebecca* again or stay home and watch "All in the Family"?

"Nothing would make me happier," Norwood cried.

Do not use the quotation mark for humor or to set off a cliché or well-known expression. If you want to use an expression, use it: don't apologize for it by using quotation marks.

POOR:   When it comes to candy, I'm just a gal "who can't say no"!

POOR:   He wanted a "meaningful" relationship.

Here are three rules for punctuating quotation marks.

(1) Place periods and commas *inside* quotation marks.

"My father," Edwina explained, "is an inventor."

(2) Place colons and semicolons *outside* quotation marks.

Milton writes of the "twilight shade of tangled thickets"; he is referring to the death of paganism.

Last year, I re-read Willa Cather's story "Paul's Case": it still stunned me.

(3) Place dashes, question marks, and exclamation marks *inside* the quotation marks when they apply to the quoted matter. Place them *outside* when they apply to the whole sentence.

Father asked, "Are you going to Alaska?"

Have you seen any episodes of "Upstairs, Downstairs"?

---

## EXERCISE

Revise these sentences, deleting faulty punctuation and adding punctuation where necessary. Revise words when necessary.

1.  We played handball; and then we swam fifty laps.

2.  "Not with a bang, but a whimper;" thus wrote Eliot.

3.  Mort Thompson, he was called Jenkins then, was a counterfeiter and con artist.

4.  There are three examples of the confined heroine in fairy tales, Cinderella, Sleeping Beauty, Rapunzel.

5.  He was a very "laid-back" character.

6.  What do you think of Pope's "The Rape of the Lock?"

7.  F. Scott Fitzgerald was a midwesterner at Princeton; and later wrote about the experience.

8.  "Nothing in the novel" he declared, "supports your opinions".

---

## Capitalization

1. Capitalize the first word of every sentence.

   Wildflowers may be grown in the garden. Rationing is an unpleasant word for most Americans.

2. Capitalize proper names—the names of people, places, and things.

   Tom and Jerry

   Nevada

   Abraham Lincoln

3. Capitalize words derived from proper names.

   Shakespearean

   Edwardian

   New Yorker

4. Capitalize words used as an essential part of proper names.

   Pueblo High School

   Fifth Avenue

   Central Park

   Lake Champlain

   but:

   The high school is on the south side.

   The avenue is the site of a parade.

   The park is in the middle of the city.

   The name of the lake is Champlain.

5. Capitalize the names of institutions and organizations.

   University of Chicago

   Department of Interior

   Office of City Planning

   The Boy Scouts of America

   Boston Red Sox

6. Capitalize words pertaining to the Deity and names of sacred texts.

> Holy Scripture
>
> Koran
>
> the Bible
>
> God
>
> the Lord

7. In titles, capitalize the first and last word and all other words except *a, an, the,* and short conjunctions and prepositions. Capitalize longer prepositions or conjunctions.

> *The Wind in the Willows*
>
> *The Man Without a Country*
>
> "Stars Fell on Alabama"
>
> "Love Among the Ruins"

8. Capitalize titles before a name, and titles of high rank appearing alone.

> President Johnson
>
> the President
>
> the Prime Minister
>
> Queen Victoria
>
> Dr. Smith
>
> Private Wilson

but:

> The president of the company is very rich.
>
> He is a private in the army.

9. Capitalize periods of history.

> the Middle Ages
>
> the Renaissance
>
> the Baroque period

Do not capitalize the name of a century.

> the nineteenth century

## EXERCISE

Supply the proper capitalization for the sentences below.

1. She is comparing the language of the bible to the language of the dead sea scrolls.

2. He attended the university of iowa before taking a job with the central intelligence agency.

3. He went to college in florida for two years and then he switched to Kenyon college.

4. I walked down main street and turned off onto one of the sidestreets.

5. During the ceremony, the governor sang "beautiful ohio" with Mayor sorenson.

6. Have you read Jane Austen's *Sense and sensibility*?

7. The enlightenment was an eighteenth-century european movement characterized by skepticism.

8. She knows by heart Browning's poem, "the bishop orders his tomb at saint praxed's church."

# A Checklist of Sixty-five Frequently Misspelled Words

| | |
|---|---|
| absence | definitely |
| abundance | disastrous |
| accommodate | effect |
| achievement | embarrass |
| acquire | fascinate |
| all right | height |
| arguing | its (possessive pronoun) |
| beginning | it's (it is) |
| burial | necessary |
| comparative | occasion |
| conscious | occurred |
| particular | transferred |
| personal | unnecessary |
| personnel | undoubtedly |
| possession | unusually |
| practical | using |
| precede (come before) | vacuum |
| proceed (advance) | vengeance |
| prejudice | warrant |
| principal | weather (rain) |
| privilege | whether (or not) |
| psychology | weird |
| recommend | writing |
| referring | written |
| reminisce | who's (who is) |
| roommate | whose (possessive pronoun) |
| rhythm | yield |
| sense | your |
| separate | you're (you are) |
| their (possessive pronoun) | |
| there (signifying place) | |
| they're (they are) | |
| theories | |
| to | |
| too (also) | |
| two (number) | |

# Sample Term Paper With Annotations*

*See page 108 for annotations keyed to the sample paper.

# MAINSTREAMING HANDICAPPED

# CHILDREN

In recent years, the rights of the handicapped have gained

public attention.   Legislation has been passed to ensure equal rights

A  in employment opportunities and pay, equal access to transportation

and buildings, and equal educational opportunities.   One of these

laws is Public Law 94-142, The Education for All Handicapped

Children Act of 1975, which was fully implemented in September,

1978.   P. L. 94-142 has made mainstreaming mandatory in public

schools.   Mainstreaming is the term used to describe the practice

of educating handicapped and nonhandicapped students together.

Despite difficulties, mainstreaming is considered to be a desirable

and workable system for educating handicapped children.

B        Public Law 94-142 defines handicapped children as the men-

tally handicapped, hard of hearing, deaf, bone impaired, health

impaired, speech impaired, visually handicapped, seriously emo-

tionally disturbed, and those with specific learning disabilities.[1]

---

[1] Alan Abeson and Jeffrey Zettel, "The End of the Quiet
Revolution, "Exceptional Children, 44 (October 1977), 123.

In the past, handicapped children were excluded from public schools by law and policy. Parents either kept their children at home or sent them to institutions. It was not until the late 1940s that an effort was made to provide special educational services for handicapped

C children. These services consisted of self-contained classrooms and schools, segregated from mainstream education. In this way, administrators and teachers got rid of problem children in the classroom, and handicapped students were thought to receive needed "separate but equal" education. It was an example, as Edwin W. Martin points out, of the "out-of-sight/out-of-mind syndrome."[2]

D But educators and teachers began to question the efficiency and validity of self-contained classrooms and schools. In the 1950s and 1960s, increasing discontent with the system's failures found a voice in Lloyd Dunn's groundbreaking article, "Special Education for the

E Mildly Retarded--Is Much of it Justifiable?"[3] Dunn's work was "symptomatic of growing disenchantment with emerging practices of special education."[4]

---

[2] Edwin W. Martin, "Some Thoughts on Mainstreaming," in Mainstream Currents, ed. Grace T. Warfield (Reston, Va.: Council for Exceptional Children, 1974), p. 2.

[3] Grace T. Warfield, ed., Mainstream Currents (Reston, Va.: Council for Exceptional Children, 1974), p. iii.

[4] Garry W. Hammons, "Educating the Mildly Retarded: A Review," in Mainstream Currents, ed. Grace T. Warfield (Reston, Va.: Council for Exceptional Children, 1974), p. 33.

F    First of all, Dunn seriously doubted the efficiency of segregated schooling. He cited research which suggested that emotionally disturbed children did as well in regular classrooms as in special classrooms and that retarded students did as well or better.[5] In addition, Dunn distrusted the process of labeling a child "mentally retarded." Too often, he thought, the label prejudiced the teachers and gave the child low self-esteem. The label becomes a "destructive, self-fulfilling prophecy."[6] Finally, Dunn claimed that recent changes in schools themselves made special classes less justifiable. Increased

G    team teaching, flexible grouping, new teaching machines, and better trained teachers meant more flexibility in the classroom. That flexibility could accept the handicapped.[7]

Alan Abeson and Jeffrey Zettel sum up the arguments against labeling and segregating handicapped children.[8] They claim that

H    handicapped children wear their labels as a badge of disgrace. The label causes them to be rejected by other children and school personnel. Stuck with the label, the child conforms to it--that is, he

---

[5] Lloyd Dunn, "Special Education for the Mildly Retarded--Is Much of It Justifiable?" in Mainstream Currents, ed., Grace T. Warfield (Reston, Va.: Council for Exceptional Children, 1974), p. 10.

[6] Ibid., p. 11.

[7] Ibid., p. 12.

[8] Abeson and Zettel, pp. 118-119.

fails. Thus, the label isolates the child and the special classes complete the process by isolating the child from usual school opportunities. Finally, some students (like the physically handicapped) do not need special education. And some labeling may be incorrect. For example, children for whom English is a second language may be incorrectly labeled as mentally retarded.

In short, the system's failures resulted from the following:

> . . . the exclusion of children who have handicaps, incorrect or inappropriate classification, labeling, or placement, and the provision of inappropriate education programs, as well as arbitrary decisions.[9]

In order to adjust these practices, the United States Congress designed P. L. 94-142. In a statement of findings and purposes, the Congress particularly addressed the problem of isolating handicapped children:". . . one million of the handicapped children in the U. S. are excluded entirely from the public school system and will not go through the educational process with their peers."[10]

Public Law 94-142 guarantees all children a free and appropriate education. Education Digest describes an appropriate education as "building educational programs to fit the child rather than simply fitting the child into existing programs."[11]

---

[9] Abeson and Zettel, p. 117.

[10] Ibid

[11] "Education for the Handicapped," Education Digest, 43 (October 1977), 12.

As Dean C. Corrigan points out, for years educators had talked about individualized education, but P. L. 94-142 required it. [12]

Does P. L. 94-142 demand that all children be mainstreamed, regardless of handicap? No. The law provides alternatives to main-streaming if that would be more beneficial to the child. [13] Public schools must mainstream only children who will benefit more from regular education than from segregated classrooms or schools.

J    Arthur Kraft, a psychologist for a school district in California, states that the decision to segregate a child in special education classes "is based on whether or not he is apt to be segregated in his adult life." [14] If a child is ultimately to hold a job in regular society and function as an independent adult, then placing him permanently in a segregated classroom does little to prepare him for his adult life. Most mildly handicapped children fit into this category; for them, mainstreaming is the answer.

---

[12] Dean C. Corrigan, "Public Law 94-142," in Teacher Education, eds. Judith K. Grosenick and Maynard C. Reynolds (Minneapolis: University of Minnesota, 1978) p. 19.

[13] Thomas H. Powell, "Educating All Disabled Children: A Practical Guide to P. L. 94-142." The Exceptional Parent, 8 (August 1978), 5.

[14] Arthur Kraft, "Down with (Most) Special Education Classes!" Academic Therapy, 8 (Winter 1972-73) 209.

Of all handicapped children, the ones that educators might hesitate most to mainstream are the mildly retarded--the educable

K mentally retarded, or EMR. But in fact this group may be successfully mainstreamed. Harold D. Love, a special educator, defines the EMR child as one with an IQ of approximately 50-75. He explains that after these children leave school, they usually hold jobs and function as normal adults.[15]

L Regular classroom placement has been shown to be a viable

M alternative for these EMR children. For example, a study on the effects of integrating EMR children was conducted in California by several professors and school officials. In this study, the progress of both EMR and normal children in the integrated classroom was compared to the progress of separate groups of handicapped and nonhandicapped children. Children in both categories of the integrated groups made as much or more progress as those in the segregated classrooms.[16]

N Similar results were found in another study conducted in

O Dallas. Two groups of EMR children were studied. The groups were closely paired according to handicap, behavior, gender and

---

[15] Harold D. Love, Educating the Exceptional Child in the Regular Classroom (Springfield: Charles C. Thomas, 1972), pp. 26-27.

[16] Robert H. Bradfield, et. al., "The Special Child in the Regular Classroom," Exceptional Children, 39 (February 1973), 384-390.

ethnic origin.  One group was integrated and the other was placed in special classes.  The results showed that the majority of the integrated children were well adjusted and that they progressed academically as well as or better than their counterparts in the segregated classrooms.  In addition, the mainstreamed children were able to participate in school activities usually unavailable to children in self-contained classrooms, such as athletics and school clubs.[17]

P        But if mainstreaming is beneficial to children, it also requires special measures to make it work.  For example, EMR children cannot simply be placed in a regular classroom and left alone with any extra help.  Kraft suggests that the EMR child can have one less

Q    subject and that he could receive tutoring in his other subjects from better students.  He adds that tutoring is good for the tutors as well as to those getting the tutoring.[18]  Lita Schwartz suggests stimulating the children's interest with audio-visual equipment like a tape recorder

R    or closed-circuit television.  And a trip to the local fire station is a concrete way to teach social studies.[19]

---

[17] Daniel J. Macy and Jamie L. Carter, "Comparison of a Mainstream and Self-contained Special Education Education Program," Journal of Special Education, 12 (Fall 1978)  303-312.

[18] Kraft, p. 210.

[19] Lita Linzer Schwartz, The Exceptional Child, Belmont, California: Wadsworth Publishing Company, Inc., 1975), p. 27.

S        The emotionally disturbed child can also benefit from mainstreaming. Jack Powell, an educator, makes several suggestions for coping with an emotionally disturbed child in the classroom. He suggests that the teacher praise positive behavior rather than merely

T    punishing negative behavior. In addition, he points out that these children are more easily frustrated than other children, and the teacher should provide means for the child to relieve his frustration.[20] Kraft comments that some children may need to spend part of the day in a "resource room," learning skills that will help them cope when they go back to the classroom.[21] Resource rooms, staffed by special educators, can be used for a variety of handicapped children. EMR children, for example, can go there to receive help in a specific subject, such as math or reading.[22]

U    The easiest of all handicapped children to mainstream are those with physical handicaps. Adjustments must be made if mainstreaming is to be successful. Adaptations in the school's structure may be

V    necessary. Provisions for wheelchairs, such as ramps, adjusted chairs, and bathroom facilities, will be needed. A quiet corner might

---

[20] Jack Powell, "Mainstreaming Eight Types of Exceptionalities," Education, 99 ( Fall 1978), 57.

[21] Kraft, p. 211

[22] Macy and Carter, pp. 311-312.

be set aside for some children. For example, the cerebral palsied child with uncontrolled movements may need times of rest and quiet.[23]

For the hearing impaired child, the teacher can give special visual emphasis--for example, a list of new vocabulary words on the blackboard which would be a help to everyone in the class. The teacher should talk at a moderate rate and face the class when speak-

W ing to aid lip-reading students. The hearing impaired child can be assigned a friend to take notes for him. The friend can also repeat information when necessary.[24] For the visually impaired, open shelving for Braille books and Braille typewriters can be provided. Storage areas can be labeled in Braille. An abacus, tape recorder, and manual materials like pegboards and puzzles are useful. The other children in the classroom must push in chairs and keep the room straight to insure easier mobility.[25]

For the most part, physically handicapped students fit into regular classrooms very well. After a while, everyone adjusts to

X the child's needs and limitations. One example is a boy paralyzed from the waist down since birth. He was integrated into a kindergarten

---

[23] Bonnie B. Greer and Jo Allsop, "Adapting the Learning Environment for Hearing Impaired, Visually Impaired, and the Physically Handicapped," <u>Exceptional Children</u>, 39 (February 1973), 250-252.

[24] Greer and Allsop, pp. 188-191

[25] Ibid. pp. 188-191.

class in Tennessee. During the day, the boy often slipped out of the wheelchair and played with the other children on the floor, pulling himself about with his arms. When one visitor came to the classroom, the child was on the floor with the other children. As the visitor left, he remarked, "I'm sorry the mainstreamed child wasn't here today. I really wanted to see how things were working out for him."[26]

Y The students in the classroom play an important role. Mainstreaming will not be successful if they reject the handicapped child. Their attitudes depend a great deal on the attitudes of their teachers. A teacher should not overemphasize a handicap. But at the same time, he should not pretend it does not exist. Special educator Kathleen Dunlop, states that children are aware of physical and behavioral differences. Avoiding discussion of these differences doesn't make them go away. In fact, such avoidance makes children think that the differences are bad or unfortunate.[27] Furthermore, as Shirley Cohen asserts, "Fear of the handicapped is often fed by lack of information or misinformation."[28] Teachers should be willing to explain why a certain child can't see or why another child is in a wheelchair.

---

[26] Kathleen H. Dunlop, "Mainstreaming: Valuing Diversity in Children," Young Children, 32 (May 1977), 31.

[27] Ibid., p. 29.

[28] Shirley Cohen, "Improving Attitudes Toward the Handicapped," Education Digest, 43 (March 1978), 18.

Z          And studies have shown that mainstreaming does change

children's attitudes for the better.  One California study tested

children's view of physically handicapped children before and after

mainstreaming.  The results showed that the children's attitudes

became more positive after integration.[29]

AA          Finally, however, it is the teacher who must make main-

streaming work.  Unfortunately, many administrators and teachers

have had little experience with the handicapped.  Teachers must be

taught to instruct the handicapped in the regular classroom.  Educa-

tion majors must be required to take courses on the handicapped and

their educational problems.  Teacher training programs, Corrigan

suggests, should be practical and emphasize the human aspect of

teaching.[30]

BB          Teachers need support of different kinds to succeed.  They

need guidance in the special instruction for the handicapped.  They

need information on useful new materials.  They need the opportunity

to develop and test new ideas.[31]

---

[29] Jacqueline Rapier, et. al., "Changes in Children's Attitudes Toward the Physically Handicapped, "Exceptional Children, 39 (November 1972), 219-223.

[30] Corrigan, p. 26.

[31] Schwartz, p. 129.

CC In addition, they should be able to discuss their problems with others.

Cohen suggests that workshops and discussion groups be held for the

adults in the school system.[32] Special educators should run the

workshops. Talking problems over with experienced educators may

help reduce teachers' anxieties about teaching the handicapped.

The rights of the handicapped, as Dean Corrigan says, is

really a matter of human rights.[33] Mainstreaming handicapped

children is a way of seeing them as citizens with educational rights--

DD and not as misfits, who must be hidden away. In fact, mainstream-

ing should apply to more than education. Whenever possible, it

should be the goal of all handicapped children and adults to live in

a fully integrated society.

---

[32] Cohen, pp. 16-18.

[33] Corrigan, p. 18.

# BIBLIOGRAPHY

Abeson, Alan, and Jeffrey Zettel. "The End of the Quiet Revolution." Exceptional Children, 44 (October 1977)

Bradfield, Robert H., et. al. "The Special Child in the Regular Classroom." Exceptional Children. 39(February 1973)

Cohen, Shirley. "Improving Attitudes Toward the Handicapped." Education Digest, 43(March 1978)

Corrigan, Dean C. "Public Law 94-192." Teacher Education. Edited by Judith Grosenick and Maynard C. Reynolds. Minneapolis: University of Minnesota, 1978.

Dunlop, Kathleen H. "Mainstreaming: Valuing Diversity in Children." Young Children, 32(May 1977)

Dunn, Lloyd. "Special Education for the Mildly Retarded--Is Much of It Justifiable?" Mainstream Currents. Edited by Grace T. Warfield. Reston, Va.: Council for Exceptional Children, 1974.

"Education for the Handicapped." Education Digest, 43(Oct. 1977)

Greer, Bonnie B., and Jo Allsop. "Adapting the Learning Environment for Hearing Impaired, Visually Impaired, and the Physically Handicapped." Exceptional Children.

Hammons, Gary W. "Educating the Mildly Retarded: A Review." Mainstream Currents. Edited by Grace T. Warfield. Reston, Va.: Council for Exceptional Children, 1974.

Kraft, Arthur, "Down with (Most) Special Education Classes!" Academic Therapy, 8(Winter 1972-73)

Love, Harold D. Educating Exceptional Children in Regular Classrooms. Springfield: Charles C. Thomas, 1972.

Macy, Daniel J. and Carter, Jamie L. "Comparison of a Mainstream and Self-contained Special Education Program." Journal of Special Education, 12(Fall 1978)

Martin, Edwin W. "Some Thoughts on Mainstreaming." Mainstream Currents. Edited by Grace T. Warfield, Reston, Va.: Council for Exceptional Children, 1974.

Powell, Jack. "Mainstreaming Eight Types of Exceptionalities." Education, 99 (Fall 1978)

Powell, Thomas H. "Educating All Disabled Children: A Practical Guide to P. L. 94-142." The Exceptional Parent., 8(Aug. 1978)

Rapier, Jacqueline, and et. al. "Changes in Children's Attitudes Toward the Physically Handicapped." Exceptional Children. 39(Nov. 1972)

Schwartz, Lita Linzer. The Exceptional Child. Belmont, California: Wadsworth Publishing Company, Inc.

Warfield, Grace T., ed. Mainstream Currents. Reston, Va.: Council for Exceptional Children, 1974.

# *Annotations: Mainstreaming Handicapped Children*

A  Introductory paragraph gives brief background. Also, definition of a central term. The thesis statement is clearly stated in the last sentence.

B  Another central term is defined. A reliable source of the definition is cited.

C  Recent history of educating handicapped children is given.

D  Transitional word *but* at beginning of paragraph shows contrast to preceding paragraph.

E  Direct quotations from Martin and Dunn concise and to the point.

F  Transitional phrases move this paragraph along, making it easy to follow: first of all, in addition, finally.

G  Generalization about "recent changes" is supported by specific examples: "increased team teaching," etc.

H  Repetition of words—label and labeling—is a good transitional device in the paragraph. Note also transitional words: thus, finally, and.

I  Important definition from a reliable source.

J  Good description of a source.

K  Important definition given.

L  First sentence in paragraph supports thesis statement.

M  Generalization followed by specific example and introduced clearly by transitional phrase: for example.

N  The phrase *similar results* clearly relates this paragraph to the one that went before it.

O  A second specific example is given.

P  Transitional *but* clearly shows contrast to what went before.

| | |
|---|---|
| Q | Supports thesis idea that mainstreaming can be made to *work*. |
| R | Good concrete and specific examples. |
| S | First sentence in paragraph supports the thesis statement. |
| T | Good specific examples from two sources given for coping with an emotionally disturbed child. |
| U | Note progression in term paper from most difficult children to mainstream (mentally retarded) to easiest children to mainstream (the physically handicapped). In this way, the writer can conclude with the most positive evidence. |
| V | Good concrete and specific examples. |
| W | Good examples from two sources. |
| X | Excellent example which makes the practice of mainstreaming very real for the reader. And, because it's positive evidence in support of mainstreaming, the example supports the thesis statement. |
| Y | This evidence supports the thesis idea that mainstreaming can be made to work. |
| Z | This evidence supports the thesis idea that mainstreaming is desirable. |
| AA | Note transitional phrases: finally, however. |
| BB | The problems of teaching mainstreamed children is treated fairly. But evidence is presented in a positive way; it shows that the problems have solutions and that mainstreaming can be made to work. |
| CC | Transitional phrases: repetition of *they need, in addition*. |
| DD | The conclusion in brief. It emphasizes the basic view of the writer—that the handicapped should be integrated, rather than segregated. |

# Index

# NOTES

# NOTES

# NOTES

# NOTES

# NOTES

# NOTES

# NOTES

# NOTES